SECOND EDITION

STUDENT WORKBOOK

WRITING WITHIN CRIMINAL JUSTICE

WRITE & WRONG

CAROLINE W. FERREE

HEATHER L. PFEIFER
School of Criminal Justice
University of Baltimore

JONES & BARTLETT
LEARNING

World Headquarters
Jones & Bartlett Learning
5 Wall Street
Burlington, MA 01803
978-443-5000
info@jblearning.com
www.jblearning.com

Jones & Bartlett Learning books and products are available through most bookstores and online booksellers. To contact Jones & Bartlett Learning directly, call 800-832-0034, fax 978-443-8000, or visit our website, www.jblearning.com.

> Substantial discounts on bulk quantities of Jones & Bartlett Learning publications are available to corporations, professional associations, and other qualified organizations. For details and specific discount information, contact the special sales department at Jones & Bartlett Learning via the above contact information or send an email to specialsales@jblearning.com.

Copyright © 2018 by Jones & Bartlett Learning, LLC, an Ascend Learning Company

ISBN: 978-1-284-11299-3

All rights reserved. No part of the material protected by this copyright may be reproduced or utilized in any form, electronic or mechanical, including photocopying, recording, or by any information storage and retrieval system, without written permission from the copyright owner.

The content, statements, views, and opinions herein are the sole expression of the respective authors and not that of Jones & Bartlett Learning, LLC. Reference herein to any specific commercial product, process, or service by trade name, trademark, manufacturer, or otherwise does not constitute or imply its endorsement or recommendation by Jones & Bartlett Learning, LLC and such reference shall not be used for advertising or product endorsement purposes. All trademarks displayed are the trademarks of the parties noted herein. *Write & Wrong: Writing Within Criminal Justice Student Workbook, Second Edition* is an independent publication and has not been authorized, sponsored, or otherwise approved by the owners of the trademarks or service marks referenced in this product.

There may be images in this book that feature models; these models do not necessarily endorse, represent, or participate in the activities represented in the images. Any screenshots in this product are for educational and instructive purposes only. Any individuals and scenarios featured in the case studies throughout this product may be real or fictitious, but are used for instructional purposes only.

Production Credits
VP, Executive Publisher: David D. Cella
Executive Editor: Matthew Kane
Associate Acquisitions Editor: Marisa A. Hines
Director of Vendor Management: Amy Rose
Director of Marketing: Andrea DeFronzo
Marketing Manager: Lindsay White
Manufacturing and Inventory Control Supervisor: Amy Bacus
Composition and Project Management: S4Carlisle Publishing Services
Cover Design: John Pfeifer/Kristin E. Parker
Rights & Media Specialist: Robert Boder
Media Development Editor: Shannon Sheehan
Cover Image: © John Pfeifer
Printing and Binding: Edwards Brothers Malloy
Cover Printing: Edwards Brothers Malloy

6048

Printed in the United States of America
22   10 9 8 7 6

Dedication

In memory of my mother, who always believed in me.
—Caroline Ferree

To my husband, John, and my daughters, Emily and Audrey.
—Heather Pfeifer

Contents

Preface xi
Foreword xiii
Acknowledgments xv

UNIT 1 Introduction 1

Introduction 2
Writing a Paper: An Overview 2
    Academic Writing: General Rules 2
    The Importance of Good Content and Good Presentation 3
Library Research: An Overview 4
    The Research Paper: Primary Versus Secondary Research 4
    Academic (Scholarly) Sources 4
    Identifying Academic (Scholarly) Sources 5
    Nonacademic Sources 5
    Rules to Follow for Selecting Sources 6
    Suggested Databases for Library Research 6
Two Styles of Papers 7
    The Analytical Paper (Informative Paper) 7
    The Argumentative Paper (Persuasive Paper) 8
Introduction, Handout #1 17
Introduction, Handout #2 19

UNIT 2 Criminal Justice Library Research 21

Performing Library Research: An Overview 22
Getting Started: Research Maps 22
    Creating a Research Map 22
Conducting Criminal Justice Library Research 24
    Criminal Justice Abstracts 25
    ProQuest Criminal Justice 27
    National Criminal Justice Reference Service (NCJRS) 29
    Bureau of Justice Statistics (BJS) 30
    National Institute of Justice (NIJ) 31
Criminal Justice Library Research, Handout #1 35
Criminal Justice Library Research, Take-Home Assignment #1 43
Criminal Justice Library Research, Take-Home Assignment #2 45

Contents

UNIT 3   Plagiarism   47

Plagiarism: A Definition and an Overview of the Problem   48
   Prevalence of Plagiarism   48
   The Three Most Common Forms of Plagiarism   49
   Why Students Plagiarize   49
Rules for Avoiding Plagiarism   49
   General Rule   49
   Specific Rules for Avoiding Plagiarism   50
   Review of Actions That Constitute Plagiarism and Cheating   52
Paraphrasing Material   53
   Paraphrasing Statistics   53
   Rewriting Comparisons Across Groups   54
   Accurately Paraphrasing Information Through Note-Taking   55
Plagiarism, Class Exercise #1   59
   Identifying Plagiarism, Part I   59
Plagiarism, Class Exercise #2   63
Plagiarism, Class Exercise #3   65
Plagiarism, Class Exercise #4   67
Plagiarism, Handout #1   69

UNIT 4   Organizing a Paper: From Taking Notes to Creating an Outline   71

Organizing an Academic Paper: An Overview   72
Taking Notes   72
   Taking Notes for the Informative Section of a Paper   72
   Taking Notes for the Persuasive Section of a Paper   74
Creating an Outline   75
   General Format of an Outline   75
   Creating an Outline from the Notes   76
Organizing a Paper, Handout #1   83
   Sample Outline   83
Organizing a Paper, Take-Home Assignment #1   89

UNIT 5   Mechanics of Writing: From the First Draft to the Final Paper   91

Academic Writing: An Introduction   92
Writing an Academic Paper: General Rules   93
Writing an Academic Paper: From the First Draft to the Final Draft   93
   Getting Started: Writing the First Draft   94
   Writing and Editing the Second (and Subsequent) Drafts   94
Assembling Your Final Paper: From the Title Page to the Reference List   109
   Creating a Title Page   109
   Creating a Running Head With Page Numbers   110
   Attaching the Reference List   110
Proofreading Your Paper: The Final Step   110
   Proofreading: General Rules   110
   Proofreading Your Paper: A Checklist   111
Mechanics of Writing, Class Exercise #1   115
Mechanics of Writing, Class Exercise #2   119

Contents   vii

    Mechanics of Writing, Class Exercise #3   121
    Mechanics of Writing, Class Exercise #4   123
    Mechanics of Writing, Class Exercise #4   125
    Mechanics of Writing, Class Exercise #5   127
    Mechanics of Writing, Handout #1   129
    Mechanics of Writing, Handout #2   131
    Mechanics of Writing, Handout #3   133
    Mechanics of Writing, Handout #4   137
    Mechanics of Writing, Handout #5   139
    Mechanics of Writing, Take-Home Assignment #1   141

UNIT 6   Writing an Annotation   143

    Writing an Annotation: An Overview   144
    Rules for Writing an Annotation   145
    Two Types of Commonly Annotated Criminal Justice Sources   145
        Empirical Studies   145
        Research Reports   146
    Approach to Writing an Annotation   146
    Writing an Annotation, Class Exercise #1   151
    Writing an Annotation   155
    Writing an Annotation, Take-Home Assignment #1   159

UNIT 7   Creating a Reference List in APA Style   163

    APA-Style Reference List: An Overview   164
    Citations on the Reference List   164
        Citing Authors   165
        Citing the Date of Publication   166
        Citing the Title of a Journal Article   167
        Citing the Title of a Journal   167
        Citing the Volume and Issue Numbers   168
        Citing the Pages of a Journal Article   168
        The Finished Citation   168
    Citations for Different Types of Sources   169
        Print Sources   169
        Electronic Sources   171
    Creating a Reference List in APA Style, Class Exercise #1   175
    Creating a Reference List in APA Style, Handout #1   179
    Creating a Reference List in APA Style, Handout #2   181
    Creating a Reference List in APA Style, Take-Home Assignment #1   183

UNIT 8   Citing in the Text in APA Style   185

    Citing in the Text in APA Style: An Overview   186
    Citing a Source at the End of a Sentence   187
        General Rules   187
        Citing One Author   187
        Citing Two Authors   187

Citing Three, Four, or Five Authors   188
Citing Six or More Authors   189
Citing a Government Agency   189
Citing Multiple Sources ("String" Citations)   189
Incorporating a Citation Into a Sentence   191

General Rules   192
Citing One Author   192
Citing Two Authors   194
Citing Three, Four, or Five Authors   195
Citing Six or More Authors   196

Combining In-Sentence Citations With Citations at the Ends of Sentences   197

Miscellaneous Rules for Citing in the Text   198

Citing a Secondary Source   198
Incorporating a Quote Into a Sentence   198

Citing in the Text in APA Style, Class Exercise #1   203
Citing in the Text in APA Style, Class Exercise #1   205
Citing in the Text in APA Style, Class Exercise #2   207
Citing in the Text in APA Style, Handout #1   211
Citing in the Text in APA Style, Handout #2   213

UNIT 9 Preparing for the Job Market   215

Writing a Résumé: An Overview   216
Writing a Résumé: The Basic Rules About Appearance   217
Writing a Résumé: The Basic Rules About Content   217
Writing a Résumé: Getting Started   218

Education Information   218
Employment Information   218
Certifications and Technological Skills   218
Academic and Professional Honors   218
Community and Professional Engagement   219

Writing a Résumé: The Details   219

The Appearance   219
The Specific Sections   220

Writing a Cover Letter: An Overview   226

The Importance of Writing a Good Cover Letter   227
Specific Tips to Follow When Writing a Cover Letter   227
Electronic Communications: An Overview   228

Tips for Drafting a Professional Email   228

Professional Social Media Profiles: An Overview   229

The Negative Impact of an Unprofessional Social Media Profile   230
Creating a Professional Social Media Profile   230

Preparing for the Job Market, Handout #1   235
Preparing for the Job Market, Handout #2   239
Preparing for the Job Market, Handout #3   241
Preparing for the Job Market, Take-Home Assignment #1   243

Contents

UNIT 10 Preparing Professional Reports and Presentations   245

    Writing in a Professional Setting: An Overview   246
    Writing in the Criminal Justice Profession   246
        Incident Reports: An Overview   246
        Risk Assessment Instruments: An Overview   248
        Child Protective Services Intake Form: An Overview   250
    Preparing a Professional PowerPoint Presentation: An Overview   251
        Guidelines for Creating and Delivering a PowerPoint Presentation   251
    Preparing Professional Reports and Presentations, Handout #1   273
    Preparing Professional Reports and Presentations, Handout #2   277
    Preparing Professional Reports and Presentations, Handout #3   281
    Preparing Professional Reports and Presentations, Handout #4   283
    Preparing Professional Reports and Presentations, Handout #5   285
    Preparing Professional Reports and Presentations, Take-Home Assignment #1   291
    Preparing Professional Reports and Presentations, Take-Home Assignment #2   293
    Preparing Professional Reports and Presentations, Take-Home Assignment #3   295

References   297

Preface

This workbook is designed specifically to help criminal justice students improve their research and writing skills. It can be used as a class text and as a reference guide for students to use outside of class. By using this workbook, students will learn how to find academic sources through library research, how to organize research material and use it to write a paper that follows APA Publication Manual (6th edition) rules, and how to create a reference list for a paper. This workbook will also help students prepare for entering the job market, by discussing how to write a professional résumé and cover letter, how to prepare PowerPoint presentations, and how to write a variety of professional reports.

To help students practice the different research and writing skills that are covered in this workbook, most of the units include handouts that they can refer to when working on a paper, as well as exercises that will help them to practice the skills that were introduced in that unit. In addition, each unit in the workbook includes fill-in-the-blank examples for students to answer. Finally, at the end of each unit there are blank pages on which the students can write notes.

For some students, this workbook will serve as the main text for a research and writing course that they must complete within their specific degree program. As such, there are handouts and class exercises included at the end of each unit. For other students, this workbook will be used as an ancillary to the main text. In this case, the instructor will incorporate one or more of the units from this workbook into his or her regular course content to teach specific research and writing skills (e.g., plagiarism, APA rules of citation). Because the instructor might teach only specific units, he or she will tell the students which handouts and which units to use.

An *Instructor's Manual* (978-1-2841-2427-9) is available for adopting institutions and contains lectures corresponding to the chapters of the **Student Workbook**. Every lecture includes detailed lesson plans, Notes to the Instructor, PowerPoint presentations, in-class exercises with answers, and reference guides. Also contained in this in-depth teaching tool are a sample syllabus, grading rubrics, homework assignments with answers, and a midterm exam with answers.

Foreword

Very few people enjoy writing. Organizing what you want to say and presenting it in a coherent manner that conveys to the reader what you mean is hard work. Writing well is extremely difficult, because it requires a lot of time and mental effort, as well as an ability to view one's own work critically. I have written many manuscripts in my 20-plus years in academe, and I can promise you that I never sat down at my computer and said, "Boy, I sure am looking forward to spending the next two (or four or eight) hours writing! I'd much rather be writing than playing basketball or watching television or eating or cleaning the bathroom."

But just as cleaning the bathroom is something that must be done, writing is a task that college students and criminal justice professionals must do. Everyone has to write, because writing is one of the primary ways by which we communicate with each other. Writing is especially important in large organizations, where it is not possible to simply speak to everyone who needs to hear what you have to say. Students must be able to communicate with their professors in order to demonstrate that they have mastered a subject. Police officers have to write accident reports and warrant applications. Probation and parole officers have to write reports. Lawyers must write briefs.

Writing well is an essential skill in the professional world, including criminal justice. So how does one become a good writer? The same way a person becomes a great guitar player: practice, practice, and more practice. This means writing, rewriting, receiving feedback, and revising what you have written based on this feedback. Your professors do not make you write because they enjoy reading what you write. (If you think writing is hard, you should try editing someone else's writing!) However, professors continue to give students writing assignments, so there must be a reason, assuming it is not their desire to suffer and see you suffer. The reason is that they recognize that good writers are not born with that talent; they acquire it. To be a good writer, you must write and write and write some more. You must have your writing evaluated by others so you can see what you are doing well and what you are not doing well.

Which brings us to this wonderful little book you hold in your hands. It has no doubt been assigned as reading for a class in criminal justice, perhaps a "writing intensive" class or "senior seminar" class that emphasizes writing. When you picked it up from the shelf at the bookstore, you might have thought to yourself, "Jeepers, I am a criminal justice major—I understand the need to read books that deal with one of the aspects of the criminal justice system, but a book about writing? Oh, boy." Well, before you set it aside, I encourage you to examine the table of contents and give some thought to what I have to say in this Foreword. There is much that you can learn in these 300 or so pages that will help you both in college and in your career.

If you are skeptical about what I have to say, ask the next criminal justice professional you encounter whether writing matters. I have had many criminal justice professionals (including police officers, probation and parole officers, correctional officers, and lawyers) speak to my classes over the years, and I always ask them what is the most important skill that a person entering their profession needs. They invariably mention the ability to communicate, both orally and in writing.

So it is not just your professors (whom you, perhaps mistakenly, assume enjoy writing) who will tell you that writing is an essential skill; those who are out working in the "real world" will tell you the same thing.

Use this book to become a better writer. Everything you need to improve your writing—in your criminal justice classes and beyond—is here. And know that if you work at it, you will become a better writer. Becoming a better writer is not easy, but it is possible if you are willing to put in the time. And remember, there are real, tangible benefits to taking the time to work on improving your writing. Good writers get better grades on papers, and they receive better grade point averages. Good writers get noticed by their superiors in criminal justice agencies, and they are rewarded with promotions. Writing matters.

Craig Hemmens, JD, PhD
Department of Criminal Justice & Criminology,
Washington State University

Craig Hemmens is Chair and Professor in the Department of Criminal Justice & Criminology at Washington State University. He holds a JD from North Carolina Central University School of Law and a PhD in Criminal Justice from Sam Houston State University. Professor Hemmens has published 20 books and more than 200 articles and other writings on a variety of criminal-justice-related topics—and Bruce Springsteen. He has served as editor of the *Journal of Criminal Justice Education* and as President of the Academy of Criminal Justice Sciences.

Acknowledgments

I would like to thank Kim Wiklund for her endless patience, continuing support, and unwavering sense of humor throughout the course of the writing of this book. Her contributions were invaluable. I would also like to thank my coauthor, Heather, for asking me to help her grade student papers over a decade ago, which set into motion the creation of a research and writing class for criminal justice students and, ultimately, this manual.

— Caroline Ferree

I would like to thank my mentor, David Barlow, for helping me discover my love of teaching and encouraging me to write this manual. I would also like to thank my graduate assistant, Vickie Sneed, for assisting in pulling together the new material for the second edition. Most importantly, I would like to thank my coauthor, Caroline, for remaining in the trenches with me and helping bring this project to fruition.

— Heather Pfeifer

We would also like to thank the following individuals who reviewed the manuscript:

James Blair, South Texas College
Bobby Craven, Bartow Criminal Justice Academy
Jim Dudley, San Francisco State University
Aric W. Dutelle, University of Wisconsin-Oshkosh
Sara Ellen Kitchen, Chestnut Hill College
Connie M. Koski, Longwood University
Gina Robertiello, Felician University
Kathy Sperry, PhD, Texas Technical University

Introduction

UNIT 1

UNIT SUMMARY
Learning Objectives
Introduction
Writing a Paper: An Overview
    Academic Writing: General Rules
    The Importance of Good Content and Good Presentation
Library Research: An Overview
    The Research Paper: Primary Versus Secondary Research
    Academic (Scholarly) Sources
    Identifying Academic (Scholarly) Sources
    Nonacademic Sources
    Rules to Follow for Selecting Sources
    Suggested Databases for Library Research
Two Styles of Papers
    The Analytical Paper (Informative Paper)
        Writing an Analytical Paper
    The Argumentative Paper (Persuasive Paper)
        Narrowing the Scope of a Topic
        The Thesis Statement
            How to Write a Thesis Statement
        The Problem Statement
            How to Write a Problem Statement
    Writing a Policy Paper

Learning Objectives

At the end of this unit, students will be able to do the following:
- State the general rules about academic writing.
- Identify academic sources and the databases in which to find them.
- Identify the differences between analytical (informative) and argumentative (persuasive) papers.
- Narrow the scope of an overly broad topic.
- Create a thesis statement for an argumentative (persuasive) paper.
- Write a problem statement for an argumentative (persuasive) paper.
- Identify the information to include when writing a policy paper.

Introduction

Using the Student Workbook, you will learn how to write a paper in an academic style. Specifically, you will learn how to find academic sources through library research, organize the materials, and use proper grammar and mechanical rules to write a paper and reference list in accordance with the *Publication Manual of the American Psychological Association* (APA), *Sixth Edition*. You will also learn how to write different types of professional correspondence, including a résumé, a cover letter, and professional email inquiries. In addition, you will learn tips on how to create a professional social media profile to help you be better prepared when you enter the job market. Finally, you will learn how to prepare a PowerPoint presentation, as well as several field reports, including a police report, a risk/needs assessment instrument, and a child protective services report.

Writing a Paper: An Overview

As a criminal justice student, you may be asked to write several different types of papers and prepare a variety of reports. When you complete these assignments, you must write in an academic style. How to write in an academic style will be covered in detail in Unit 5, "Mechanics of Writing: From the First Draft to the Final Paper," but for now, here are a few general rules.

Academic Writing: General Rules

Academic writing is more formal than other writing styles.
- Do not use contractions.
- Do not use slang. One example of slang is writing "kid" instead of "child."

> **Example:**
>
> Write two examples of slang you should not use and the correct words you should use in their place.
> _____
> _____

- Do not use flowery language; state things simply and clearly. One example of a sentence written using flowery language is, "The attorney's closing argument was wonderfully eloquent and strong." This should be written more simply as, "The attorney's closing argument was strong."

Writing a Paper: An Overview

> **Example:**
> Write an example of flowery language and the correct (simple) way to write it.
> _____
> _____

- Present all of the information in a neutral and objective tone; you must not include your personal opinions. Thus, you should not use "I," "my," "we," "us," or "our."
- Include only information that comes from academic sources, not from your own knowledge.
- Cite all of your sources in your paper in APA style, consistent with the *Publication Manual* (6th edition). You will learn how to do this in Unit 8, "Citing in the Text in APA Style."
- Create a reference list, prepared in APA style, consistent with the *Publication Manual* (6th edition). It must include all of the sources you cite in your paper. You will learn how to do this in Unit 7, "Creating a Reference List in APA Style."

The Importance of Good Content and Good Presentation

In addition to writing your paper in an academic style, you must also concentrate on the content and presentation of your writing. An effective paper must be strong in both. To understand what this means, imagine the two scenarios in the following example.

> **Example:**
>
> **Scenario #1:** *You go to a wedding where there is a beautiful cake. It has fluffy, white frosting with lots of colorful flowers. It is perfectly shaped and looks spectacular. However, when you are given a piece to eat, it is dry and has no flavor. You are disappointed, because it looked so good that you thought it would taste equally great.*
>
> **Scenario #2:** *A little girl wants to make her mother a birthday cake. With the help of her father, she follows a recipe for a chocolate cake. She insists on frosting and decorating the cake herself. When she is finished, it is lopsided and the frosting is uneven. But it tastes delicious.*

How do each of these scenarios compare with writing a paper that has both good content and good presentation? In the first scenario, the presentation is excellent, but the content is poor. This can describe a paper that is well written but that lacks content. For example, the grammar and mechanics might be correct, but it is missing important information or it contains only a superficial discussion of the topics.

In the second scenario, the presentation is poor, but the content is good. This can describe a paper that has the essential information (content) but has poor grammar or many mechanical errors. In this scenario, the paper might be hard to follow because the errors distract the reader from the content.

The bottom line is that neither of these papers is going to earn a good grade! A good paper must be strong in both content and presentation.

By using the Student Workbook, you will learn how to construct a paper that is strong in both content and presentation. You will also learn how to do library research to find the information you need to write your paper and to present that information in a well-organized, well-written manner that is consistent with the citation standards of the *Publication Manual* (6th edition).

Library Research: An Overview

One type of paper you may be asked to write is a research paper. Students are often confused about what this means. It is important that you understand what a research paper is so that you will know how to write one when you are assigned to do so. It is also important that you know how to conduct library research to find the best sources for your paper. This information will be covered in detail in Unit 2, "Criminal Justice Library Research" but we will discuss some general information about it here.

The Research Paper: Primary Versus Secondary Research

When you write a *research paper*, you will summarize and critique research that has been conducted by other people. In other words, you will formulate a thesis statement (which you will learn how to do later in this unit) and do library research to find published literature on your topic. You will then read and summarize that information. This is called *secondary* research. It is different from *primary* research, in which researchers collect and analyze data, make findings about it, and draw conclusions from it. Typically, scholars in the field write papers using primary research.

For the purposes of this workbook, the terms "research" and "library research" mean the same thing.

Academic (Scholarly) Sources

When you do your library research for your paper, you should obtain your information only from academic sources unless your instructor tells you otherwise. An academic source is also known as a "scholarly source." It is empirically based; that is, it is grounded in research and is not simply someone's personal opinion. Moreover, an academic source is one that has been "peer reviewed" by experts in the field for its accuracy and quality. Some examples of academic sources are as follows:

- *Peer-reviewed journal articles.* These are articles that have been "cleared" by scholars in the field before publication. For example, when an author sends an article to the editor of a journal to be published, that editor does not decide whether to publish it or not. Instead, he or she sends it out to several reviewers who read it, make comments, ask questions, and make publication recommendations. Sometimes the reviewers also recommend certain changes that should be made before it is published. The reviewers then send their reports to the editor, who contacts the author. These same steps are followed for the publication of grant proposals and research reports. Three examples of peer-reviewed journals are *Justice Quarterly, Criminology,* and *Crime & Delinquency.*
- *Scholarly books.* These are good resources because they often present a wide range of information on a topic written by experts in the field. A scholarly book can be a summary of multiple authors' (or a single author's) own research, or it can be a volume of related essays—similar to an anthology—written by several authors and compiled into a book by an editor(s).

Examples:

Cook, P. J., & Goss, K. A. (2014). *The gun debate: What everyone needs to know.* Oxford: Oxford University Press.

Adelsberg, G., Guenther, L., & Zeman, S. (Eds.). (2015). *Death and other penalties: Philosophy in a time of mass incarceration.* New York: Fordham University Press.

To determine if a book is scholarly, read the preface or introduction to see if it lists the authors' credentials (e.g., PhD) or affiliations with educational institutions or government agencies. If the authors' credentials or affiliations are stated, it is probably a scholarly book.

- *Research reports published by government agencies.* Two good sources for research reports are the National Institute of Justice (NIJ), which is the research arm of the U.S. Department of Justice, and the Bureau of Justice Statistics (BJS). The BJS will likely have any crime-related statistic you require. Other good sources for research reports are state government agencies that have a publishing or research department, as well as independent social research agencies.
- *Law review articles.* Published by law schools, law review articles are a good source if your topic is law related. However, their scope is typically limited because their focus is exclusively on the law.
- *White papers.* A white paper presents an agency's or organization's social or political position on a particular issue. Its purpose is to educate the public on how and why the agency views the issue the way it does. White papers occasionally make recommendations on how an agency thinks an issue should be handled.

For example, in March 2011, the White House released a white paper that addressed the issue of the sale of counterfeit drugs through online pharmacies. This paper included recommendations on how Congress could help curb the problem by passing more stringent legislative penalties (Espinel, 2011).

Identifying Academic (Scholarly) Sources

Sometimes you will not know if a source is academic (scholarly). In such cases, there are certain things you can check to help you determine whether it is a scholarly source.

- *Names of authors.* Scholarly sources have named authors. If an article is attributed to "Anonymous," it is not scholarly.
- *Length.* A scholarly article is typically 5–30 pages long. If the article is very short (e.g., one page), it is not scholarly.
- *Pictures.* Scholarly articles typically do not have pictures.
- *Reference list.* Scholarly articles are research articles, and, as such, the authors must include a reference list of their sources. If an article does not have a reference list, it is not scholarly.
- *Biographies.* Scholarly journals often include author biographies. Nonacademic journals do not. Note, however, that you should not rely solely on this factor to determine whether the source is scholarly, because not all scholarly articles include biographies.
- *Credentials (e.g., JD, PhD) after the authors' names.* As with biographies, scholarly journals often list author credentials; however, they do not *always* do so. Again, you should not rely solely on this factor to determine whether a source is scholarly.

Nonacademic Sources

Nonacademic sources do not require the same in-depth review process that academic sources do. In fact, some sources, such as Wikipedia, allow anyone to post an entry, and there is no oversight to check the accuracy and reliability of the information. Accordingly, you should *not* use any of the following to write your papers unless your instructor approves their use:

- magazines (e.g., *Newsweek, Time, U.S. News & World Report*);
- newspapers (e.g., *New York Times, Washington Post*);
- encyclopedias or Wikipedia;
- textbooks; or
- trade journals (e.g., *Police Chief*).

There are two exceptions to this list:

1. You can use encyclopedias specific to criminal justice or criminology, such as the *Encyclopedia of Crime & Justice*, the *Encyclopedia of Criminology*, and the *Encyclopedia of Crime and Punishment*. These academic resources provide overviews of specific topics that relate to crime and the criminal justice system, and using them may help you better understand your topic.
2. When you write an academic style paper, you can use a recent case profiled in the news to introduce your topic. For example, if you are writing a paper in which you argue that the death penalty should be abolished, you may use a recent newspaper article about an inmate who was freed from death row because new DNA evidence exonerated him. You could also use a magazine article that discusses problems that states have had with lethal injection executions. However, remember that this type of information comes from nonacademic sources. Therefore, check with your instructor first to ensure it is an appropriate source for you to use.

Rules to Follow for Selecting Sources

As you do your library research, there are several ways to ensure that you find the best sources for your paper.

- *Read abstracts.* Abstracts give you a summary of the article or report, which will allow you to determine whether it is on point with your research question or thesis statement.
- *Focus on current research.* Criminal justice research is continuously evolving, so you should limit your research to the most current research available. A good rule of thumb is to find sources published within the past 10 years unless your instructor tells you otherwise.
- *Focus on current statistics.* When you write your paper, you should present the most recent statistics available that are related to your topic. Note, however, that in some instances, the most "recent" statistics are not very current. For example, there is approximately an 18-month lag in the annual criminal statistics published by the FBI (*Uniform Crime Reports*).
- *Keep it in the United States.* Unless you are writing a paper on an international topic or are comparing a U.S. policy or practice with that of another country's, you should use research that has been conducted only in the United States.

Suggested Databases for Library Research

When you conduct your library research, you should do so in criminal-justice-related databases and websites only, unless you instructor tells you otherwise. Students often use databases such as Wikipedia and search engines such as Google and Yahoo! to conduct their library research. However, there is little oversight of these websites and search engines, and entries may be made by anyone. Thus, most of the information contained in them is not academic and should not be used when you write your research paper.

A few good databases and websites that you can and should use include the following:

- *Criminal Justice Abstracts*
- *ProQuest Criminal Justice*
- National Criminal Justice Reference Service (NCJRS)
- Bureau of Justice Statistics (BJS)

We will discuss in detail how to navigate these databases in Unit 2, "Criminal Justice Research."

Note! Although there are many good criminal justice databases and websites to use for criminal justice research, do not limit yourself to these sites. Many criminal justice issues are multidisciplinary, and you can find criminal-justice-related research in the works of other disciplines such as psychology, sociology, and education. For example, if you are writing a paper on school violence, you could conduct a search in the education databases, such as Education Resources Information Center (ERIC), as well as in the criminal justice databases. Moreover, different disciplines approach topics from different angles and, therefore, may provide you with valuable information. If you do use databases from other disciplines, remember to use your checklist to determine whether the articles you have found are scholarly.

Two Styles of Papers

There are two styles of academic papers: the *analytical* paper (sometimes referred to as an *informative* paper) and the *argumentative* paper (sometimes referred to as a *persuasive* paper). The purpose of both types of papers is to educate the reader.

The Analytical Paper (Informative Paper)

An analytical paper is sometimes referred to as an informative paper because it informs the reader about a topic. In this section, we will refer to it as an "analytical" paper.

When you write an analytical paper, you will choose a topic, write a question about it that interests you, present a summary of the literature on that topic, and state a conclusion to your question. Importantly, when you write this style of paper, you will not just "regurgitate" the literature. Instead, you will critically assess it and, using that information, draw your conclusion. Moreover, you will not try to "persuade" your reader to adopt one point of view or another; you will merely present your information neutrally and then state *your* conclusion based upon the literature.

Writing an Analytical Paper

The first step in writing an analytical paper is to state your topic; this is usually done in the form of a question. For example, if you are interested in writing about drug courts, your question may be, "Do drug courts offer a viable alternative to incarceration for nonviolent offenders?"

After you have created your question, your next step will be to educate your reader about your topic. The best way to do this is to find (and use) academic sources that answer the following questions: Who? (or What?), Where?, When?, and Why?

> **Example:**
> You are writing a paper about drug courts. Using information drawn from the literature, you could discuss what they are (definition), who they are designed to help, who is involved in the courts (e.g., attorneys, social workers), how they are incorporated into various states' judicial systems, when they were created, and why they were created.

After you have educated your reader, your final step will be to write your conclusion. In it, you will answer your research question and state any future implications. When you do this, remember that you are writing *your* position. You should not try to sway your reader to adopt it.

Example:

You have decided that drug courts are beneficial for drug offenders who have not been charged with violent crimes. You could write, "Drug courts are a viable alternative for nonviolent offenders. Therefore, more resources should be allocated to these programs so that offenders can receive treatment in the community rather than in jail."

> **Note!** When you write your conclusion, do not write, "I think that drug courts are a viable alternative to incarceration for nonviolent offenders." The word "I" should not appear in your paper. Instead, simply write, "Drug courts are a viable alternative for nonviolent offenders."

The Argumentative Paper (Persuasive Paper)

An argumentative paper is sometimes referred to as a persuasive paper because it attempts to persuade the reader to adopt the writer's position on an issue. In this section, we will refer to it as an "argumentative" paper.

When you write an argumentative paper, you will choose a position on a debatable issue relating to the topic and will argue that position by presenting empirical studies that support your argument. In general, an empirical study is one in which researchers have analyzed data from which they have made findings and drawn conclusions. Although there may be strong arguments that are contrary to your chosen position, you should acknowledge them and then present your research in a manner that will refute those arguments.

> **Note!** When you write an argumentative paper, take a position but do not include your personal opinion. As with an argumentative paper, the word "I" should not appear in your paper.

Narrowing the Scope of a Topic

In some classes, you may be asked to write an argumentative paper on a very broad topic (e.g., "female offenders"). If you were to attempt to write a paper on such a broad topic, your library research would result in thousands of hits (search results)—an overwhelming amount of information. Therefore, you must narrow the scope of the topic before you start your library research. Moreover, by narrowing the scope of your topic, you will be better able to formulate your thesis statement. We will discuss in more detail how to write a thesis statement in the next section.

To narrow the scope of your topic, follow these steps:

1. *Brainstorm!* On a piece of paper (or in a Word document), list all of the answers you can think of to the following questions:
   a. *Who?* In other words, what types of females are there (e.g., age, race, ethnicity, role)? One example of a type of female is Hispanic mothers.

Example:

Write three examples of different types of females.

_____

_____

_____

Two Styles of Papers

b. *What?* In other words, what types of offenders are there (e.g., drug offenders, violent offenders, sex offenders)?

Example:
Write three examples of different types of offenders.
_____
_____
_____

2. Combine some of the elements from both lists to create a type of female offender.

Example:
Write three examples of different types of female offenders.
_____
_____
_____

3. Once you have a specific type of female offender in mind, ask yourself what you are interested in learning about this population. For example, "Why might they engage in that behavior?" or "What is the community or criminal justice system doing to prevent or control the behavior?" This will help you begin to formulate your research question or thesis statement.

Example One:
You are interested in writing about adolescent female gangs. Ask yourself what you want to learn about them. For example, you might want to learn why girls join gangs. To learn why, you could explore the literature to find what risk factors have been identified in girls who join gangs. You could also explore the literature to identify programs that have been developed to prevent girls from becoming involved in gangs or that target young female gang members and focus on helping them get out of that lifestyle.

Example Two:
You are interested in writing about drug-addicted mothers. Ask yourself what you want to learn about them. For example, you might want to learn how the mother's drug addiction affects her ability to care for her children. Or you might want to examine how the drug addiction affects the mother–child bond and whether those mothers are more likely to abuse or neglect their children. If you choose this topic, you could conduct library research to determine what programs exist to help these women.

Note! When you choose a topic for a paper, choose something that interests you. It is easier to write a paper about something you care about than to write a paper about something that bores you.

The Thesis Statement

When you write an argumentative paper, you must include a thesis statement. A thesis statement is a one-sentence statement that tells your reader what your paper will be about.

How to Write a Thesis Statement

When you write a thesis statement, you should follow these rules:

- It must be specific and narrow.
- It cannot be a question.
- It must be a debatable issue for which research has been conducted. It cannot be a statement of fact or an opinion.
- You must pick a side of the debatable issue; do not be ambiguous.

Once you have narrowed the scope of your topic and determined what you are interested in learning about that particular type of offender, you can write a thesis statement. However, before you write a thesis statement, you should do some preliminary research about your topic so that you become familiar with it. This will make it easier to write your thesis statement.

When you do your preliminary research, you will look for the answers to particular questions.

Example:

Assume you have narrowed the scope of your topic to "juvenile female gang members." You would research the following questions:

- *Why?* Why do those offenders engage in the particular activity? For this example, you would look for answers to the question, "Why do juvenile females join gangs?" In other words, what risk factors are associated with juvenile females joining gangs (e.g., drug use, childhood abuse, peer pressure)?
- *How?* How can the behavior be stopped? For this example, you would look for programs, policies, or intervention strategies that have been established to help young female gang members leave the gangs (e.g., drug treatment programs for youth, job-training programs).
- *What?* What changes do we expect to see? For this example, you would look for discussions about the behavioral changes of young female gang members who participate in a drug treatment program or who are affected by a policy.

Once you have considered each question, you can put your findings together into a thesis statement.

Example:

A thesis statement for a paper about juvenile female gang members might be, "Adolescent females who have a history of maltreatment are more likely to become involved with gangs to feel a sense of security, a sense of belonging, or both."

Note! After you start your library research, you may discover that there is too much information about your topic or that there is not enough. In either instance, you should edit your thesis statement. If there is too much information, you should try narrowing your thesis statement further. If there is too little information, you may want to broaden your thesis statement.

Two Styles of Papers

In-Class Practice

Narrow the scope of the topic of juvenile delinquency and write a thesis statement for it.

_____
_____
_____

The Problem Statement

When you write an argumentative paper, your instructor may ask you to write a problem statement for the paper. A problem statement is a paragraph that describes a problem you believe needs to be addressed and sets forth a solution for that problem. When you write a problem statement, you must clearly articulate for the reader what the problem is and must discuss why it is important that it be addressed.

How to Write a Problem Statement

Before you write your problem statement, you must first think of a problem that needs to be addressed. Examples of problems you could address include prison overcrowding, the disproportionate representation of minorities in correctional populations, and the increasing number of juveniles waived to the adult system. When you select a problem, remember that it must be one that can be resolved!

Once you have determined the problem that you will address, you can begin to draft your problem statement. There are three parts to a problem statement: (1) the vision statement, (2) the issue statement, and (3) the solution statement.

The first part of the problem statement—your vision statement—is the opening sentence of your paragraph. It describes what the ideal scenario would be if your problem were remedied.

> **Example:**
>
> In your problem statement, you will address the problems that sexual assault victims may encounter in the criminal justice system after reporting an assault. Specifically, they are often treated poorly by the criminal justice system. Your vision of an ideal scenario for these victims might be that they would feel safe and comfortable enough to report the assault, and that professionals would be available to help them navigate the criminal justice system. Accordingly, the first sentence of your problem statement (the vision statement) might read:
>
> *"When victims of sexual assault seek assistance from the criminal justice system, they expect that the professionals they encounter will treat them with compassion and respect and will help them navigate the various processes in the system."*

The second part of your problem statement is the issue statement. This will be longer than your vision statement and will consist of several sentences that describe the problem in its current state. Thus, for the previous example, you would describe what the situation is really like for sexual assault victims who report their crimes.

Before you write your issue statement, you should spend some time thinking about the answers to the following questions:

1. Whom does the problem affect (e.g., specific people, communities, agencies)?

    In this example, it affects sexual assault victims.

2. What does the problem affect (e.g., what is its impact)?

    In this example, it affects the victims' willingness to report assaults.

3. When does the problem occur (e.g., at what time, during what processes)?

   In this example, it occurs when the victims report assaults and as they move through the legal process. Specifically, victims could be asked to repeat their stories several times to different people. Also, they might not be told what to expect from the system, might not be kept apprised of how their case is progressing, and might not be told why certain decisions are made.

4. Where is it a problem (e.g., only in certain places, instances)?

   In this example, it is a problem in hospitals, other medical facilities, police stations, and courts.

5. Why is it a problem (e.g., What are the consequences, and why is it important that we fix it?)? In this example, it is a problem because it may make victims feel retraumatized. It also may make them less willing to report a crime and less willing to help with their own cases.

> **Note!** When you write your issue statement, you should also try to include some statistics (national, state, or local) that can help further illustrate the scope of the problem.

The final part of your problem statement is your solution statement. This section will be a few sentences that describe how you think the problem can be resolved. As with the previous sections, you should think about various solutions to your problem before you draft the solution statement. For example, you could discuss a new policy or practice, or suggest a new intervention that could be created to resolve the problem.

> **Example:**
>
> You have concluded that a way to resolve the problems sexual assault victims encounter when they report an assault is to provide them with a professional who will help them (a victim's advocate). The advocate would be assigned to a victim when he or she first reports the crime and would help the victim through each step until the case is resolved. Your solution statement would briefly describe how the victim's advocate would help the victim feel less traumatized and would thereby improve his or her satisfaction with the system.

Once you have completed each of these steps, you will use that information to write a concise paragraph. As with all formal writing, you should write several drafts of the problem statement. You should not write only one draft.

> See **Introduction, Handout #1: "Sample Problem Statement"** at the end of this unit.

Writing a Policy Paper

One type of analytical paper you may be asked to write is a policy paper in which you must discuss the effectiveness of a program or policy. When you write this type of paper, there is specific information you should include in it. In the first part of the paper, you should educate your reader about your program or policy. To do this, you should include the following:

- a description of the policy or program,
- the scope of the problem it is trying to address,
- its history,

Two Styles of Papers

- its purpose or goals,
- the population targeted, and
- its activities or elements.

When you discuss the history, you should include information about its origins, as well as the context within which the program or policy was created.

Note! If you are asked to write a policy paper, some examples of criminal justice policies you could write about are mandatory arrest for domestic violence, capital punishment, and sex offender registry laws. A few examples of criminal justice programs you could write about are problem-solving courts, DARE, and Neighborhood Watch programs.

Hint! When you write your policy paper, you should discuss each element in the order in which it is listed in "Writing a Policy Paper" section. Doing so will ensure that your paper is well-organized.

In the second part of the paper, after you have educated the reader about the policy or program, you should summarize a few empirical studies that have examined its effectiveness. For each study, you should summarize the research question, identify the population examined, and discuss how the data were obtained, as well as the findings and any significant limitations. When you write this part of the paper, discuss each study separately; do not lump them all together into one paragraph.

See **Introduction, Handout #2: "Writing Assignment: Research Paper"** at the end of this unit.

NOTES

Introduction, Handout #1

Sample Problem Statement

When victims of sexual assault seek assistance from the criminal justice system, they expect that the professionals they encounter will treat them with compassion and respect and will help them navigate the various processes in the system (vision statement). According to the Rape, Abuse, and Incest National Network (RAINN, 2009), approximately 213,000 individuals are sexually assaulted every year. Yet, according to data compiled by the Bureau of Justice Statistics, only 35% of sexual assault victims report such incidents to law enforcement (Truman & Langton, 2014). This is because those who do decide to seek the help of the criminal justice system often find the experience to be both frustrating and traumatic. Specifically, victims are asked to repeatedly recount the details of their assault to numerous people. In addition, they may not be informed about what decisions are made relating to their case or why these decisions are made. These experiences may cause victims to feel retraumatized. Consequently, victims may cease to cooperate with criminal justice professionals or they may refuse to seek the assistance of the system in the future (issue statement). By providing these individuals with a sexual assault victim's advocate after they initiate contact with the system, the advocate can help minimize the victims' feelings of isolation and improve their satisfaction with the system. Further, advocates can help victims navigate and understand the legal process and serve as a liaison between the victims and the other professionals who work in the system (solution statement).

Introduction, Handout #2

Writing Assignment: Research Paper

For this class, you will write a 7- to 10-page research paper on one of the topics approved by your instructor. The purpose of the paper is to provide the reader with a synopsis of the policy's or program's history, purpose, goals, target population, and activities or elements; thus, you must include the following information in your paper:

- a description or definition of the program or policy, including a brief discussion of the scope of the problem (e.g., statistics) that the policy or program is trying to address;
- a discussion of the history of the program or policy, including why, where, and when it was created;
- a discussion of the purpose(s) or goal(s) of the program or policy (i.e., what it is designed to accomplish, who or what it is targeting); and
- a discussion of the elements of the program, including activities or actions designed to accomplish the program's goals.

In addition, you must summarize three empirical studies that have evaluated how effective the program or policy has been in achieving its goals. For each study, you must include the following information:

- a summary of the research question examined,
- a summary of the population examined,
- a summary of how the data were obtained (i.e., the type of information collected),
- a summary of the findings as they relate to the thesis statement (e.g., evidence the author[s] found that supports it), and
- a brief discussion of any significant limitations to the findings.

All information contained in the paper must come from academic sources unless your instructor tells you otherwise. In addition, you should *not* rely on your own knowledge about the topic. Moreover, you must use a minimum of *eight* academic sources when writing your paper. Your paper must be written in APA format and must include citations written in APA format. *Failure to include citations constitutes plagiarism.* Your paper must include a title page as well as a reference page. (Neither the title page nor the reference page will count toward the 7- to 10-page requirement.) Points will be deducted from papers that do not meet the page requirement or that do not incorporate eight academic sources.

Complete photocopies of *all* sources noted on the final reference list must be turned in with your paper. Papers that do not include photocopies of all of your sources will *not* be accepted.

Criminal Justice Library Research

UNIT 2

UNIT SUMMARY
  Learning Objectives
  Performing Library Research: An Overview
  Getting Started: Research Maps
    Creating a Research Map
  Conducting Criminal Justice Library Research
    Criminal Justice Abstracts
      Conducting Research Using a Research Map
      Conducting Research Without Using a Research Map
    ProQuest Criminal Justice
      Conducting Research Using a Research Map
      Conducting Research Without Using a Research Map
    National Criminal Justice Reference Service (NCJRS)
      Conducting Research Using a Research Map
      Conducting Research Without Using a Research Map
    Bureau of Justice Statistics (BJS)
      Conducting Research in BJS
    National Institute of Justice (NIJ)
      Conducting Research in NIJ

Learning Objectives

At the end of this unit, students will be able to do the following:

- Create and use a research map to find on-point articles.
- Successfully navigate several criminal justice databases and websites to find scholarly sources.

Performing Library Research: An Overview

Libraries provide many types of resources for your research. The information is available in hard copies, such as books, journals, magazines, and reports, as well as in a variety of online sources. As with any new skill, learning how to do library research takes time, practice, and patience! If you have been using search engines such as Google or Yahoo! to conduct your research, you will find that using a discipline-specific database (such as *Criminal Justice Abstracts*) will seem very difficult at first. However, after you have conducted several searches in the databases and become more familiar with them, you will find that they are fairly straightforward and easy to navigate. The bottom line is that the best way to become familiar with the various databases is to play in them!

Getting Started: Research Maps

Before you start your research, spend some time thinking about the best way to approach it. A computer will search only for the exact words you select, and in the exact order you type them. Therefore, you must choose the words and their order with care so that you do not waste time reading irrelevant abstracts or articles.

> **Example:**
>
> You want to find an article that includes statistics about where prisoners go when they are released from prison. If you type "statistics about where prisoners go when they are released from prison," you will not get any hits (results). That is because the search engine will look for articles that include *all* of those words, in the same order that you typed them. To make your search more productive, you must determine the best words to use for a search and the order in which you want them to appear.

Creating a Research Map

The best way to begin your library research is to create a research map. The map is based on your thesis statement and contains the keywords you will use in your computer search, in the order in which you will use them. To create a research map, follow these steps:

1. Write your thesis statement and underline the keywords.

> **Example:**
>
> You have written the following thesis statement: *"Youths who use drugs are more likely to commit violent offenses."* To complete Step 1, you would write: "<u>Youth</u> who use <u>drugs</u> are more likely to commit <u>violent offenses</u>."
>
> _____
>
> _____

Getting Started: Research Maps

2. For each of your keywords, make a list of synonyms.

Example:

<u>Youths</u>: teenagers, adolescents, children
<u>Drugs</u>: alcohol, marijuana, heroin
<u>Violent offenses</u>: murder, rape, assault

Note! If your keyword is *drugs*, you can, and should, search for certain types of drugs. This will retrieve articles that reference a particular type of drug, but that do not use the term *drug* itself.
   In addition, you can, and should, search for specific types of violent offenses. You can also search for the phrase "violent offenses" by enclosing the phrase in quotation marks.

3. Truncate all of the words that you can. To strengthen or broaden your search, you can execute a computer search for your word along with any variations of your word that an author may have used. To do this, shorten your word to the common base it shares with the words you want to find in your computer search, and add an asterisk at the end.

Example:

You are looking for articles about teenage drug users. Because some authors may have used the word "teen" rather than "teenage," you should truncate "teenage" to "teen*." The computer will then search for "teenagers," "teen," and "teenager."

In-Class Practice: Truncating Keywords

Look at the list of synonyms we have made for the keyword "youths" in the thesis statement. Which of those words can be truncated? Where would you put the asterisks? What words will the computer look for?

_____
_____

Note! Do not shorten your word too much. If you do, it might result in the computer using words unrelated to your search and retrieving irrelevant articles. Choose carefully the best location to place the asterisk so that the computer retrieves only relevant articles.

Example:

If you initiate a search for "teenagers" and you truncate the search term as "tee*," the computer will retrieve words like "tee" and "teem."

4. Arrange your truncated synonyms into columns. To do this, write your keyword at the top of each column. Beneath each keyword, list its synonyms. This will help you visualize what you will ask the computer to find. Specifically, you will search for sources that have one of the synonyms from each column.

Example:

Youths	Drugs	Violent offenses
Teen*	alcohol	murder
Adolescen*	heroin	rape
Child*	marijuana	assault

5. Put your keywords together into a research map by stringing the synonyms in each column together with "or" and enclosing them in parentheses. Then connect each set of parenthetical information with "and."

Example:

(youth* or teen* or adolescen* or child*) and (drug* or alcohol or heroin or marijuana) and ("violent offenses" or murder or rape or assault)

In this example, the computer will find articles that have youth or teen* or adolescen* or child* *and* drug* or alcohol or heroin or marijuana *and* violent offenses or murder or rape or assault.

Note! If you find that you are not getting many hits, or that you are getting too many, there are several things you can do:
- Change your synonyms.
- Delete some of your synonyms.
- Check your spelling and the spacing between your words.
- Check where you have placed your asterisks.
- Use a different database.

In-Class Practice: Creating a Research Map

1. Using the example, "the impact of maternal drug abuse on child maltreatment," write the keywords you would use to create a research map.

   _____

   _____

2. Write the synonyms you would use for each keyword.
3. Truncate any words that would help you with your research. What other words will the computer retrieve?
4. Create your research map for this example.

Conducting Criminal Justice Library Research

When you conduct your library research, you should use only academic sources or scholarly journals unless your instructor tells you otherwise. Many of the databases have limiters, which allow you to limit your search to those types of sources. However, when you find a source, you should always make sure it is truly academic. You can determine this by using the checklist discussed in Unit 1 (e.g., the source must have named authors, be longer than a few pages, and include references). Also, when you conduct a search in any database, you should first narrow the scope of your topic, and then prepare a research map. This will make it easier for you to find relevant sources.

Note! If your instructor allows you to use nonacademic sources, he or she will discuss with you which search engines to use and how to navigate them.

There are several criminal justice databases and websites that you should use when you do library research for your paper. Remember, however, that you can also find criminal-justice-related sources in other disciplines such as psychology, sociology, and education. Therefore, if you are writing a paper on school violence, you should look in the education and psychology databases, as well as in the criminal justice databases. If you do use databases from other disciplines, remember to use your checklist to determine whether those articles are scholarly, too.

Note! As with many Internet sites, the formats of databases are frequently updated and changed. If that is the case with any of the databases we discuss in this unit, your instructor will help you navigate the changes so that you are able to find the best available sources.

Criminal Justice Abstracts

This database references criminology journals and journals of related disciplines. The full texts of many (but not all) articles are available through this database. If there is not a link to the full text of an article, you can access it by other means.

When you conduct library research in the *Criminal Justice Abstracts* database, you should begin your search in the **Advanced Search** page. There are several important features to note about this page.

- Boxes are already set up for you to enter your keywords. If you need more rows for your keywords, you can add them by clicking on the "**+**" link located to the right of the third box.
- To the right of the keyword boxes are boxes labeled **Select a Field (optional)**. These contain a drop-down menu. Click on the drop-down menu and choose the **AB Abstract or Author-Supplied Abstract** option. Other options you could choose include the last name(s) of the author(s) or the title of the article. Thus, if you have the title of the article, you can enter that in the first box, click on the drop-down menu, and choose the **TI Title** option to find your source.
- Beneath the search boxes is a section called **Search Options** with a list of options for you to choose from to conduct your search. The first option in this section is **Search modes**. Make sure the circle is set to **Boolean/Phrase**.
- Beneath the **Search Options** section is a section titled **Limit your results**. In that section, there is a **Linked Full Text** box. Clicking on this box returns results for full-text articles only. Do not click on this for your initial search because it might limit the number of results you get.
- After this there is a box labeled **Scholarly (Peer Reviewed) Journals**. If your instructor requires that you use only scholarly journals, check this box.
- The next boxes are **Publication Date** boxes. If your instructor requires you to limit your search to a certain period of time, you will use these boxes. To limit your search, using the drop-down menu, type the date you wish to start the search in the boxes on the left and the current year and month in the boxes on the right. Thus, if you have been instructed to find only articles published within the past 10 years, in the starting date box, you would type the current year, less 10.

- Below the **Publication Date** boxes, there is a box labeled **Language** with a drop-down menu that allows you to choose a language for your articles. Leave this box on the **All** setting.
- To the right of the **Publication Date** boxes is a box labeled **Publication Type**. Unless your instructor tells you otherwise, select **Academic Journal**. Finally, below the **Publication Type** box is the **Document Type** box. Unless your instructor tells you otherwise, select **Article**.

> See *Criminal Justice Library Research*, Handout #1: "Library Research Reference Guide" at the end of this unit.

Conducting Research Using a Research Map

To practice finding articles in the *Criminal Justice Abstracts* database, you will find academic sources for the phrase "teenagers who use drugs" that were published within the past 10 years. Note that if you type that phrase into the first box, you will get zero hits because the computer will search for that exact phrase. Therefore, you must use a research map to find some sources.

For this exercise, use only two synonyms per keyword. For "teenagers," type `teen*` and `youth`. For "drugs" type `drug*` and `alcohol`.

1. In the first row, type (`teen* or youth`) in the first box. (You must type the parentheses because this database does not supply them.)
2. Change the drop-down menu on the right to **AB Abstract or Author-Supplied Abstract**.
3. Leave **AND** in the connector box.
4. Type `drug* or alcohol` in the box in the second row.
5. Change the drop-down menu to the right of that row to **AB Abstract or Author-Supplied Abstract**.
6. In the **Search modes** section, select **Boolean/Phrase**.
7. Click on **Scholarly (Peer Reviewed) Journals**. Do not click on **Linked Full Text**.
8. Fill in the publication dates so that the computer will search only for articles that have been published within the past 10 years.
9. In the **Language** box, select **All**.
10. For **Publication Type**, select **Academic Journal**.
11. For **Document Type**, select **Article**.
12. Click on **Search**. This will return a list of articles. Each result will have the title of the article, a list of the subjects discussed in it, a hyperlink to the full text (if available), a hyperlink to the references cited in the article, and the option to add the result to a folder. A hyperlink, denoted in blue, allows you to go directly to that link when you click on it. For example, when you click on the hyperlink for the full text, it will pull up the full text of the article.
13. Review the list of titles until you find an article that you think will be on point with your search for "teenagers who use drugs." Click on the title of the article. This will result in an abstract page that lists the author(s), journal title, volume number, issue number, page numbers, and publication year.
14. Read the abstract carefully to make sure it is on point with your topic. If it is, click on the link to the left to view the full text of the article. If it is not on point, go back to your list and keep looking until you find a title (and then an abstract) that is on point.

Note! Not all abstracts will have links to the full text. If there is not a link to the full text, your instructor may be able to help you to determine how to obtain the full text of the article.

Conducting Research Without Using a Research Map

When you conduct library research for a particular program or policy, you will not use a research map. Instead, you will search for articles using only the name of your program or policy. If you were to use a map, you would get many unrelated hits. For example, if your topic is domestic violence courts in the United States, and you were to create the research map "(domestic or home) and (violen* or assault) and court," you would get hundreds of hits for articles that discuss many different types of violence, abuse, and assault that would be unrelated to your topic.

When you conduct library research for your paper, follow these steps:

1. In the first box on the **Advanced Search** page, enter the name of your program or policy in quotation marks (e.g., "domestic violence court*"). Do not use "and" or "or."
2. Change the drop-down menu to the right to **AB Abstract or Author-Supplied Abstract**.
3. In the **Search modes** section, select **Boolean/Phrase**.
4. Click on **Scholarly (Peer Reviewed) Journals**. Do not click on **Linked Full Text**.
5. Fill in the publication dates so that the computer will search only for articles that have been published within the past 10 years.
6. In the **Language** box, select **All**.
7. For **Publication Type**, select **Academic Journal**.
8. For **Document Type**, select **Article**.
9. Click on **Search**. This will return a list of articles.
10. Review the list of titles until you find one that is about domestic violence courts. When you find one that you think is on point, click on the title of the article. This will result in an abstract page that lists the author(s), journal title, volume number, issue number, page numbers, and publication year.
11. Read the abstract carefully to make sure it is about domestic violence courts in the United States. If it is, click on the link to the left to view the full text of the article, or consult your instructor about how to obtain the full text of the article. If it is not on point, go back to your list and keep looking until you find a title (and then an abstract) that is on point.

Note! The *Academic Search Complete* database is another good database to use. Its **Advanced Search** page is similar to that of *Criminal Justice Abstracts*. Accordingly, if you wish to do a search in *Academic Search Complete*, follow the same steps as outlined above.

ProQuest Criminal Justice

ProQuest Criminal Justice is a database with criminal justice and criminal-justice-related sources. All of the sources have links to their full texts.

As with *Criminal Justice Abstracts*, when you start a search in this database, you should begin on the **Advanced Search** page. There are several important features to note about this page:

1. The keyword search boxes in *ProQuest Criminal Justice* are similar to those in *Criminal Justice Abstracts*. However, in *ProQuest Criminal Justice*, the box to the far right defaults to **Anywhere**. Leave the keyword search boxes set to that option. As with the *Criminal Justice Abstracts* database, you can search for a source in other ways by changing the drop-down menu. In addition,

the second row allows you to use the connector "and" only once; the other connector is "or." Therefore, if you wish to add another keyword and connect it with an "and," you can do so by clicking on the **Add a row** link beneath the search boxes. If you wish to use a connector other than "and" for the second or subsequent rows, use the drop-down menu to change it.

2. Beneath the keywords search boxes are two **Limit to** boxes. The first allows you to limit your search to **Full text** and the second allows you to limit your search to **Scholarly journals**. As with *Criminal Justice Abstracts*, you should select only the **Scholarly journals** box. Do not select the **Full text** box.

3. The next option allows you to select a date range for your search. Use the drop down menu to select the dates within which you want to conduct your search. If your instructor requires you to limit your search to those articles published within the past 10 years, on the drop-down menu, select **After this date...**. Three boxes will appear. In the first box, set the drop-down menu to the current month. Leave the second box set to **Any Day**, and in the third box type the current year, less 10.

4. The next option allows you to select the **Source type**. If your instructor requires you to limit your search to academic sources, scroll down and select **Scholarly journals**.

5. To the right of the **Source type** box are options for **Document type**. If your instructor requires you to limit your search to academic journals, select **Article**.

6. The next option is **Language**. Leave it blank.

7. The next search option is **Sort results by**. Leave that box set to **Relevance**.

8. Click on **Search**.

> **Warning!** Even though you have clicked on the box limiting the results to scholarly articles, *ProQuest Criminal Justice* will sometimes retrieve articles that are not scholarly. Therefore, it is very important that you use the checklist to determine whether the article you have found is scholarly.

Conducting Research Using a Research Map

To practice finding articles in this database, you will conduct a search typing the same keywords you used with the *Criminal Justice Abstracts* database: `teen*`, `youth`, `drug*`, and `alcohol`. Again, you will limit your search to articles published within the past 10 years. To do this, follow these steps:

1. Type (`teen* or youth`) in the first box (you must type the parentheses).
2. Make sure the drop-down menu is set to **Anywhere**.
3. Leave the connector box set to **AND**.
4. On the second row, type `drug*` in the first box and `alcohol` in the second box.
5. Make sure the drop-down menu on that row is set to **Anywhere**.
6. Select **Scholarly journals** from the **Limit to** boxes.
7. Set the **Publication date** box to **After this date...** by clicking on the drop-down menu.
8. Select the month and year that will result in articles published within the past 10 years.
9. From the **Source type** boxes, select **Scholarly journals**.
10. From the **Document type** boxes, select **Article**.
11. Do not select any boxes for the **Language** options.
12. Leave the **Sort results by** box set to **Relevance**.

Conducting Criminal Justice Library Research

13. Click on **Search**.
14. This will result in a list of hits. Review the titles until you find an article that you think will be on point with your search for "teenagers who use drugs." Click on the title of the article. This will result in an abstract followed by the full text of the article.
15. Read the abstract carefully to make sure the article is on point with your topic.
16. Use the checklist to ensure that what you have found is scholarly.

Conducting Research Without Using a Research Map

Again, when you write a paper about a program or policy, you will not use a research map. Instead, follow these steps:

1. Type the term "domestic violence court*" in quotation marks in the first box.
2. Leave the drop-down menu set to **Anywhere**.
3. Select **Scholarly journals**.
4. Set the **Publication date** boxes so that your search results are limited to the past 10 years.
5. Select **Scholarly journals** as the **Source type** and **Article** as the **Document type**.
6. Do not select any boxes for **Language**.
7. Leave the **Sort results by** box set to **Relevance**.
8. Click on **Search**.
9. This will result in a list of hits that have the phrase "domestic violence court" anywhere in the article, including the title, abstract, or text. Review the list until you find an article that you think will be on point. Click on the title of the article. This will result in an abstract followed by the full text of the article.
10. Read the abstract carefully to make sure the article is on point with your topic.
11. Use the checklist to ensure that what you have found is scholarly.

> **In-Class Practice: Conducting Research in *ProQuest Criminal Justice***
>
> Using the *ProQuest Criminal Justice* database, find an article about mental health courts.

National Criminal Justice Reference Service (NCJRS)

The National Criminal Justice Reference Service (NCJRS) is a federally funded agency that offers reference and referral services about crime- and justice-related issues. In part, the NCJRS website includes abstracts for criminal justice reports, articles, books, and publications. Many of the abstracts have links to the full text of the source.

To access the NCJRS Abstracts Database, follow these steps:

1. Go to www.NCJRS.gov.
2. Click on the tab at the top of the page, **Library**.
3. Under **Resources**, click on **NCJRS Abstracts Database Search**. This will open a search page for the NCJRS Abstracts Database.
4. There are several ways you can find sources. If you are using a research map or keywords, you will use the **General Search** box. If you have the title of the article, the name(s) of the author(s), or the NCJ number, you will use one of the boxes specifically designated for that information.

As with *Criminal Justice Abstracts* and *ProQuest Criminal Justice*, NCJRS allows you to choose the dates you want the program to search by using the **Date Range** boxes.

Conducting Research Using a Research Map

This section will discuss how to conduct a search for "teenagers who use drugs" using a research map. Again, you will limit your search to articles published within the past 10 years. To do this, use the synonyms "teen*," "youth," "drug*," and "alcohol," and follow these steps:

Because the search page does not provide you with "ands," "ors," or parentheses, you will have to put them into your search.

1. In the **General Search** box, type in the research map as follows: (teen* or youth) and (drug* or alcohol). Note that you must type the parentheses.
2. Leave the **Language** box set to **ALL**.
3. In the **Date Range** boxes, type the dates that you want to search for articles and reports, but limit this to the past 10 years.
4. Select the **All** circle next to **Choose a search type**, located in the middle of the page.
5. Click on **Search**. Note that the search results page includes a variety of sources, such as journals (noted by the word "journal" and title of the journal) and reports (these have a publication date and sometimes an author's name). Note also that all of the sources have abstracts and that some have links to the source's full text.
6. Read through the list of articles returned; when you find one that you think might be on point, click on **Abstract**. Read it carefully to see if it is on point and from the United States. The NCJRS includes many sources that were published in other countries, so this check is important.

Conducting Research Without Using a Research Map

Again, when you write a paper about a program or policy, you will not use a research map. Similarly, if you want to search for a particular phrase, such as "domestic violence courts," you will do so without using a research map. To find relevant sources, follow these steps:

1. Type the name of your program or policy in the **General Search** box.
2. Select the **Phrase** circle located next to **Choose a search type** in the middle of the page.
3. Leave the **Language** box set to **ALL**.
4. Type the dates into the **Date Range** boxes so the computer searches only for sources published within the past 10 years and click on **Search**.

> **In-Class Practice: Conducting Research in NCJRS**
>
> In the NCJRS website, search for "drunk driving" using the keywords "drunk" or "drink*" and "driv*" or "auto*." How many hits did you get?

Bureau of Justice Statistics (BJS)

The Bureau of Justice Statistics (BJS) is part of the U.S. Department of Justice. It produces reports of crime-related statistics and statistical trends. To access this website, go to www.bjs.gov.

Conducting Research in BJS

There are three primary ways to find reports on this website:

The first way to find reports is as follows: On the top left-hand side is a tab called **Publications & Products**. When you click on this tab, the computer will open the **Publications & Products Overview**

Conducting Criminal Justice Library Research

page. On that page, there are several options for you to use to continue with your research. The first is to click on the **Search** link, which will open onto a page with a **Keyword** search box. Type your keywords into the box and click on **Search**. When you use the **Keyword** box, you should limit your search to general keywords, such as "child abuse" or "gangs" rather than use a research map. On the **Publications & Products Overview** page, you can also conduct a search by selecting a topic from a list (e.g., **Corrections**, **Courts**) or by selecting a product type (e.g., **Publication**, **Data Table**).

The second way to find reports is by typing keywords into the **Enter keywords** box at the top right-hand side of the page. Then, using the drop down menu in the **All Information Types** box located next to the **Enter keywords** box, click on **Publications & Products**. Then click on **GO**. When you use the **Enter keywords** box, you should limit your search to general keywords, rather than use a research map. After you type your keywords, click on **GO**.

The third way to conduct a basic search in this website is by using the menu on the left-hand side of the homepage, which lists the various topics (e.g., **Courts**, **Crime Type**). If you know which topic you need to search, click on that topic.

Example:
You need to find statistics about hate crimes Click on **Crime Type**. In the resulting drop-down menu, click on **Hate Crime**. This will bring up a page with a **Publications & Products** section listing statistical reports about hate crimes and providing hyperlinks to the reports.

In-Class Practice: Conducting a Search in BJS
In the BJS website, do a search for property crimes. What strategy did you use?

_____

_____

National Institute of Justice (NIJ)

The National Institute of Justice (NIJ) is also part of the U.S. Department of Justice. In part, it produces and sponsors reports on crime and justice. To access this website, go to www.nij.gov/.

Conducting Research in NIJ

There are three primary ways to conduct basic research on this website:

1. Type keywords into the box that is located in the top right-hand corner of the homepage. When you use this technique, you should limit your search to general keywords, such as "child abuse" or "gangs," rather than use a research map. After you type your keywords, click on **GO**. Alternatively, you can do a more advanced search by clicking on the **Advanced Search** link under the search box. This will open a page with several search boxes. In the **Publications & Multimedia** box, enter your keywords into either the **Abstracts** box or the **Full Text** box and click on **GO**.

2. Choose from a list of topics that appears on the left-hand side of the homepage.

Example:
You are conducting a search about domestic violence courts. From the list of topics, click on **Courts**. This will bring up a list of options. Click on **Specialized Problem-Solving Courts**. On the left side of the page

is a list of specialized courts. Click on **Domestic Violence Courts**. This will bring up general information about the courts, along with links to sites from which you can obtain more information about them.

3. Click on the **Publications & Multimedia** tab on the top row of the homepage. On the left side of the resulting page, there are links to various types of publications, including **Recently Published** and **Topical Collections**. Each of these links brings up a list of publications or topics from which you can choose the one you are researching. You can also use the search boxes that are in the middle of the page. In the **Title and Author Search** box, you can find a source by entering the title of your source or the name(s) of the author(s). You can also type your keywords into the **Search full text** box to find full text articles. Again, when you use this box, use only general keywords like "domestic violence courts."

Note! When you do research on this website, you must carefully read the abstracts and the PDF file, if one is available, to make sure that what you have found is a report. This website has many different types of sources, so it is important that you check to make sure what you have found is, in fact, a report.

In-Class Practice Conducting Research in NIJ

Find a report about "stalking" by using the **Publications & Multimedia** tab on the homepage.

See *Criminal Justice Library Research, Take-Home Assignment #1: "Conducting Library Research"* and *Criminal Justice Library Research, Take-Home Assignment #2: "Locating Sources for your Paper"* at the end of this unit.

NOTES

Criminal Justice Library Research, Handout #1

Library Research Reference Guide
Criminal Justice Abstracts
Conducting Research Using a Research Map

> **Example:**
> ```
> (teen* or youth) and (drug* or alcohol)
> ```

1. Type (teen* or youth) in the first box. You must type the parentheses.
2. Make sure the drop-down menu is set to **AB Abstract or Author-Supplied Abstract** in the first row.
3. Make sure the connector box is set to **AND**.
4. Type drug* or alcohol in the box in the second row.
5. Make sure the drop-down menu is set to **AB Abstract or Author-Supplied Abstract** in the second row.
6. Select the **Boolean/Phrase** circle in the **Search modes** section.
7. Select **Scholarly (Peer Reviewed) Journals**. Do *not* select **Linked Full Text**.
8. Fill in the publication dates to pull up articles published within the past 10 years.
9. Set the **Language** box to **All**.
10. Select **Academic Journal** for **Publication Type**.
11. Select **Article** for **Document Type**.
12. Click on **Search**.
13. Read through the titles until you find one that you think will be on point.
14. Click on the title.
15. Read the abstract and determine if it is on point.

Conducting Research Without Using a Research Map

> **Example:**
> ```
> DUI court*
> ```

1. Type "DUI court*" in the first box. You must use quotation marks.
2. In the drop-down menu, select **AB Abstract** or **Author-Supplied Abstract**.
3. Follow steps 6 through 15 in the previous section.

Criminal Justice Library Research, Handout #1

ProQuest Criminal Justice
Conducting Research Using a Research Map

> **Example:**
> (teen* or youth) and (drug* or alcohol)

1. Type (teen* or youth) in the first box. You must type the parentheses.
2. Make sure the drop-down menu is set to **Anywhere** in the first row.
3. Make sure the connector box is set to **AND**.
4. On the second row, type drug* in the first box and alcohol in the second box.
5. Make sure the drop-down menu is set to **Anywhere** in the second row.
6. Select **Scholarly journals** from the **Limit to** boxes. Do *not* select **Full text**.
7. Set the **Publication date** box to **After this date...** by clicking on the drop-down menu.
8. Select the month and year to retrieve articles published within the past 10 years.
9. From the **Source type** boxes, select **Scholarly journals**.
10. From the **Document type** boxes, select **Article**.
11. Do not select any boxes for the **Language** options.
12. Make sure the **Sort results by** box is set to **Relevance**.
13. Click on **Search**.
14. Read through the titles until you find one that you think will be on point.
15. Click on the title.
16. Read the abstract and determine if it is on point.

Conducting Research Without Using a Research Map

> **Example:**
> DUI court*

1. Type "DUI court*" in the first box. You must include the quotation marks.
2. Make sure the drop-down menu is set to **Anywhere**.
3. Follow steps 6 through 16 in the previous section.

Criminal Justice Library Research, Handout #1

National Criminal Justice Reference Service
(NCJRS; www.ncjrs.gov)

Conducting Research Using a Research Map

> **Example:**
> (teen* or youth) and (drug* or alcohol)

1. Click on **Library** at the top of the page.
2. Click on **NCJRS Abstracts Database Search**.
3. Make sure the **Choose a search type** circle is set to **All**.
4. In the **General Search** box, type (teen* or youth) and (drug* or alcohol).
5. Leave the **Language** box set to **ALL**.
6. Fill in the **Date Range** boxes.
7. Click on **Search**.
8. Read through the titles until you find one that you think will be on point.
9. Click on **Abstract** and read it to determine if it is on point and from the United States.

Conducting Research Without Using a Research Map

> **Example:**
> DUI court*

1. Change the **Choose a search type** circle to **Phrase**.
2. In the **General Search** box, type DUI court*.
3. Follow steps 5 through 9 in the previous section.

Criminal Justice Library Research, Handout #1

National Institute of Justice
(NIJ; www.nij.gov/)

There are several ways to do research on this website.

Method One
- Type your keywords into the box at the top right. Do *not* use a research map.
- Click on **GO**.

Method Two
- Click on the **Advanced Search** link under the search box.
- In the **Publications & Multimedia** box, enter your keywords into either the **Abstracts** box or the **Full Text** box.
- Click on **GO**.

Method Three
- From the list of topics on the left side of the homepage, click on the one that is relevant to your search.

Method Four
- Click on the **Publications & Multimedia** tab on the top row of the homepage.
- On the left side of the resulting page, click on **Topical Collections**.
- Click on the topic that is relevant to your research.

Method Five
- Click on the **Publications & Multimedia** tab on the top row of the homepage.
- Type your keywords into the **Search full text** box in the middle of the page.
- Click on **Search**.
- Click on the tab that relates to the type of report you are seeking.

Criminal Justice Library Research, Take-Home Assignment #1

Conducting Library Research

For Questions 1, 2, and 3, print out the abstract (in landscape if necessary) and write on it the search strategy you used to find the source. In writing your search strategy, do not just list the keywords. For Questions 1, 2, and 3, you must use the connectors "and" and "or" as well as parentheses and asterisks. For the first three questions, you must also use at least two synonyms for each keyword. You may use the original keywords as one of your synonyms. An example of a search strategy for "abuse of the elderly" is (abus* or harm) and (elder* or old).

1. Locate an **article** on **guns in schools** in *Criminal Justice Abstracts*. Print out the abstract and write on it your search strategy.
2. Locate an **article** on **police brutality** in *ProQuest Criminal Justice*. Print out the abstract and write on it your search strategy.
3. Locate a **report** on a **program that addresses violent adolescents** in **NCJRS**. Print out the abstract and write on it your search strategy.
4. Locate a **report** on **prostitution** in the publication database of the **National Institute of Justice**. Print out the first page of the report *and* a page from the report that shows that it is about prostitution.

Criminal Justice Library Research, Take-Home Assignment #2

Locating Sources for your Paper

1. Draft the thesis statement for your research paper. *Failure to provide a thesis statement will result in a 5-point deduction from your grade.*
2. Locate *four* academic sources that you will use for your paper.
   - *Two* sources must describe the program, address its history, or state its purpose(s) or goal(s);
   - *One* source must address the scope of the problem your program or policy is trying to fix; and
   - *One* source must be an empirical study that supports your thesis statement.

For each source, print out an abstract. Write on the abstract the topic that the source addresses.

UNIT 3

Plagiarism

UNIT SUMMARY
  Learning Objectives
  Plagiarism: A Definition and an Overview of the Problem
      Prevalence of Plagiarism
      The Three Most Common Forms of Plagiarism
      Why Students Plagiarize
  Rules for Avoiding Plagiarism
      General Rule
      Specific Rules for Avoiding Plagiarism
      Review of Actions That Constitute Plagiarism and Cheating
  Paraphrasing Material
      Paraphrasing Statistics
      Rewriting Comparisons Across Groups
      Accurately Paraphrasing Information Through Note-Taking

Learning Objectives

At the end of this unit, students will be able to do the following:

- Present an accurate definition of plagiarism and identify its most common forms.
- Avoid committing plagiarism by following general and specific rules.
- Paraphrase statistical findings into different formats (e.g., ratios, fractions, percentages, comparisons across two or more groups) to present those findings in an accurate but unique way.
- Take notes more efficiently when reviewing literature, and summarize and present that information in their own words.
- Assess what is relevant from other people's research to support their own research question or thesis statement, thereby improving their critical thinking skills.

Plagiarism: A Definition and an Overview of the Problem

Plagiarism is a form of cheating. A general definition for plagiarism is using someone else's words, ideas, statistics, or pictures and presenting them as your own. In other words, it is using another person's work without giving credit to that person. The way to give the author credit is to cite the source from which you get information.

Other forms of cheating include handing in a paper someone else has written for you; making up material, quotes, or sources; and buying a paper on the Internet.

Self-plagiarism is also cheating. You would be committing self-plagiarism if you were to hand in a paper, or portions of a paper, that you wrote for another class and present it as new work.

Prevalence of Plagiarism

Students contend that educators "make a mountain out of a molehill" when they discuss the prevalence of plagiarism. However, plagiarism is a very real problem in academics and in the professional workforce. Studies have shown that between 26% and 54% of students admit to plagiarizing (McCabe, Trevino, & Butterfield, 2001). Similarly, in a report published by the Pew Research Center, 55% of college presidents surveyed reported that the incidences of plagiarism in student papers had increased between 2001 and 2011 (Parker, Lenhart, & Moore, 2011). The problem of plagiarism exists in the workforce, too. In the past few years, there have been several highly publicized incidents of professionals who lost their jobs as a result of plagiarizing other people's work.

For example:

1. In recent years, a number of national journalists have been fired for plagiarizing the work of their colleagues (e.g., Ruth Shalit, a rising reporter with the Washington, D.C.-based paper, the *New Republic*; Jayson Blair, a national reporter with the *New York Times*).
2. A CBS news producer was fired after it was discovered that he copied a video essay from the *Wall Street Journal*.
3. A Columbia University professor was fired for plagiarizing from other people's work and passing it off as her own.
4. The principal of a Florida high school was fired for plagiarism after he delivered a speech that was written by a former student and failed to credit the student.
5. In 2006, a Harvard student named Kaavya Viswanathan authored two young adult books and received a $500,000 advance for both; she was later found to have plagiarized large passages from the works of two other famous authors of young adult books.

Rules for Avoiding Plagiarism

The purpose of this unit is to teach you how not to plagiarize so you do not commit this offense in school or in your professional career.

The Three Most Common Forms of Plagiarism

Plagiarism can be committed in several ways. The three most common forms are as follows.

1. "Cutting and pasting," which refers to cutting material (sentences, phrases, sections, or whole papers) from the Internet and pasting it into your paper, or writing down word-for-word what you read.
2. Failing to include required citations.
3. Failing to adequately paraphrase information into your own words.

Why Students Plagiarize

- *Ignorance*—Students do not know that what they are doing constitutes plagiarism.
- *Failure to understand the material*—Students find it easier to cut and paste the material than to try to understand what it means and rephrase it.
- *Poor time management*—Students wait too long to write the paper and resort to cheating to get it written on time.
- *Lack of confidence*—Students lack confidence in their research or writing abilities and are afraid to ask for help. They fear that if they turn in their own work, they will get a bad grade.
- *Lack of morals*—Students find nothing wrong with plagiarizing.
- *Lack of fear of getting caught*—Students think instructors will not catch them.
- *Poor note organization*—Students fail to make a notation in their notes that the content is verbatim from the original source and requires paraphrasing. This results in their using that verbatim information in their final paper.

Rules for Avoiding Plagiarism

You can avoid the pitfalls of plagiarizing by following some very straightforward rules; some of these rules are quite specific, but we will discuss a general rule first.

General Rule

You must completely paraphrase the material and cite the source from which you got the information. In general, paraphrasing means rewriting the information in your own words. Citing means including somewhere in your own sentence the last name(s) of the author(s) and the year the source was published. You can include the citation at the end of the sentence or incorporate it into the sentence text. You must have a citation for every paraphrased sentence.

> **Example:**
>
> Research has shown that more boys commit crimes than girls do (Wilson, 2014).
>
> or
>
> According to Wilson (2014), research has shown that more boys commit crimes than girls do.

We will discuss in detail how to incorporate citations into the text of your papers in the unit on the *Publication Manual* (6th edition) rules for citing sources in the text.

Note! You will have many citations in your paper. That is okay. It is better to have too many citations than to neglect to cite the original work. Always follow the rule, "If in doubt, cite."

Warning! Putting a citation at the end of a paragraph (as recommended by the Modern Language Association [MLA] style) without citing within that paragraph is not sufficient. Under *Publication Manual* (6th edition) guidelines, placing a citation at the end of a paragraph refers only to the information in the last sentence. In such a situation, the rest of the paragraph is plagiarized.

Specific Rules for Avoiding Plagiarism

There are several specific rules you should follow so that you do not commit plagiarism.

Rule #1: *You must cite everything that is not common knowledge.*

Common knowledge is very general information that most people in the world know (or should know). It is not information that only you know. If a piece of information is not common knowledge, you must provide a citation.

Ask yourself: Would my mother or father know this? Would my friends who are not in my field of study know this? If the answer is yes, it is common knowledge and does not require a citation. In contrast, if the answer is no, it is not common knowledge and does require a citation.

Example:

Examples of statements that are common knowledge (and do not require citations):

1. George Washington was the first president of the United States.
2. Drinking and driving is against the law.

Examples of statements that are not common knowledge (and do require citations):

1. Underage white males are more likely to drink and drive than underage white females.
2. Drunk driving offenders who participate in rehabilitation programs are less likely to recidivate.

Example:

Write two examples of statements that are common knowledge (and do not require citations):
_____
_____

Write two examples of statements that are not common knowledge (and do require citations):
_____
_____

Rules for Avoiding Plagiarism

Rule #2: *Do not just write your own thoughts.*

All of the information in your paper must come from the sources you read, and you must cite those sources. If you do just write your own thoughts, you must find sources that support those thoughts, and you must then cite those sources.

If you write your own thoughts, but the information you write is not common knowledge and you have not included any citations, you will have committed plagiarism.

Rule #3: *You must properly paraphrase the material.*

When you write your paper, you cannot just copy information from articles. Even copying one sentence is plagiarism. You must read the article and completely paraphrase the information. "Paraphrase" means to put the information in your own words.

The best way to paraphrase is to read the information in small pieces (paragraphs or portions of paragraphs), jot down keywords on a sheet of paper, and then turn the paper over. That way you will not see and, therefore, will not be tempted to use the author's words. Sit and think about what you read, and then, using your keywords, write your own paragraph.

> **Note!** When you paraphrase material from a source, you do not need to include all of the information presented in that article, chapter, or report. Just paraphrase the important information that is relevant to your topic. Also, remember that you must cite the source throughout the paragraph.

Rule #4: *Follow the list of what not to do.*

1. Do not paraphrase one sentence at a time. Read the entire paragraph and paraphrase the information in your own words.
2. Do not just change a few words or insert synonyms, and do not use a thesaurus to find alternate words to use. Not only does merely inserting synonyms constitute plagiarism, but students often choose the wrong words, thereby writing a sentence that does not make sense.

> **Example:**
> If the original sentence uses the term "six men," do not change it to "half-a-dozen men."

3. Do not just change the sentence structure by rewriting it in the passive voice.

> **Example:**
> Original sentence: *"Twelve men committed arson."*
> Rewritten into the passive voice: *"Arson was committed by twelve men."*

4. Do not just change the order of sentences.
5. Do not just leave out some of the words contained in the original source.

> **Warning!** Doing any of the above and writing a citation at the end of the sentence does not save you from committing plagiarism.

Rule #5: *Include all of the required elements for direct quotes.*

A direct quote means all the words are exactly the same. If only some of the words or phrases are identical, it is not a direct quote.

- If you want to use a direct quote that has fewer than 40 words in your paper, you must
  a. use quotation marks, *and*
  b. put a citation at the end of the quote (not after every sentence), *and*
  c. include a page number.

Failure to include all of those elements means you have committed plagiarism.

- If you want to incorporate a direct quote that is 40 words or longer, you should set it as a block quote, meaning that it should be set apart from the rest of your text in an indented paragraph. You do not need to include quotation marks, but you will need to include a citation and a page number at the end of the quote. Use a direct quote only if the information is said so spectacularly that you cannot paraphrase it. For further discussion with regard to this rule, see the *Publication Manual* (6th edition), p. 170–171.

> See **Plagiarism, Handout #1: "Rules of Plagiarism Reference Guide"** at the end of this unit.

Review of Actions That Constitute Plagiarism and Cheating

1. Copying or using a portion of another's work (such as a paper, article on the Internet, or journal article) without giving that person credit.
2. Cutting and pasting *any* amount of information from the Internet.
3. Handing in a paper that someone else wrote or that you wrote for another class.
4. Handing in a paper with portions of a paper that another student wrote or that you wrote for another class.
5. Buying a paper online.

> See **Plagiarism, Class Exercise #1: "Identifying Plagiarism, Part I"** at the end of this unit.

Follow these steps to determine if a "rewrite" of an original source is plagiarized:

1. Look at the rewrite and determine if it is a direct quote.
   a. If the answer is yes, check the rewrite for quotation marks, a page number, and a citation. If any of those are missing, it is plagiarized.
   b. If the answer is no, go through the rules of the plagiarism guide checklist (Plagiarism, Handout #1: "Rules of Plagiarism Reference Guide"). Specifically, first determine whether every sentence is cited. Second, look for the use of synonyms, language that is too close to the original, and whether the author rewrote the example sentence by sentence. Third, determine whether the author used too many of the same words from the original source in the rewrite. If citations are missing or if the answer to any of the remaining questions is yes, the rewritten work is plagiarized.

> See **Plagiarism, Class Exercise #2: "Identifying Plagiarism, Part II"** at the end of this unit.

Paraphrasing Material

When you paraphrase, you put information that you have read into your own words. Following are some guidelines for how to best paraphrase certain types of material.

Paraphrasing Statistics

Statistical information can be presented in many different ways that protect you from plagiarizing and do not require direct quotes.

1. Percentages, fractions, and decimals are all interchangeable. If you want to paraphrase a statistic that includes a percentage, you can change it into a fraction or a decimal. Similarly, if you want to paraphrase a statistic that includes a fraction, you can change it into a decimal or a percentage. Finally, if you want to paraphrase a statistic that includes a decimal, you can change it into a percentage or a fraction.

Example:
How would you rewrite the statistic 4%?
_____

2. Paraphrase statistics by approximating the numbers.

Example:
How would you rewrite 77% as an approximation?
_____

3. Paraphrase statistics by rounding them off.

Example:
How would you rewrite 2,715 as a round number?
_____

When you round off a number to paraphrase it, make sure you round to the closest and most accurate number. For example, rewriting the statistic 2,175 as "approximately 2,750" or "approximately 2,800" is misleading and inaccurate.

Note! If you are rounding off a very large number, you should put the actual number in parentheses.

Example:

If the original source states that 123 million people commit a particular offense every year, and you rewrite it as "over 120 million," you should include the actual number in parentheses at the end of the sentence: "(123 million)." Although this is not an APA requirement, it is helpful to include the actual number so that the reader does not mistakenly believe a much higher number (e.g., 200 million) commit the offense.

Rewriting Comparisons Across Groups

When you paraphrase statistics, you may have to paraphrase information that compares two or more groups. There are several different ways to present those statistics.

Example:

You are writing a term paper about the effectiveness of drug court programs. While conducting your library research, you found that approximately 30% of the males who attended the programs reoffended, and approximately 10% of the females who attended them reoffended.

	Males	Females
Percentage who reoffended	32	10.1

There are several ways to compare these two groups:

Alternative #1: Write the results as a ratio. Divide 32 by 10.1, which is approximately 3:1.

Alternative #2: Approximate the results. "Approximately 3 out of 10 (or 30 out of 100) males reoffended, and approximately 1 out of 10 (or 10 out of 100) females reoffended."

Alternative #3: Present the results as a fraction. "Approximately one-third of the males reoffended, whereas only one-tenth of the females reoffended."

Alternative #4: Compare the two. "Almost three times as many males as females reoffended."

Or present the inverse: "Approximately one-third as many females as males reoffended."

To determine which alternative is the best to use in your paper, think about your thesis statement and the point(s) you wish to make. For example, if your thesis statement is "Female offenders who participate in a drug court program are less likely to recidivate than males who participate in them," you should use the statistic that most strongly supports your position: "Females reoffend approximately one-third as many times as males."

See **Plagiarism, Class Exercise #3: "Rewriting Statistics"** at end of this unit.

Paraphrasing Material

Accurately Paraphrasing Information Through Note-Taking

Paraphrasing information after jotting down the keywords and relevant statistics is the only way you should paraphrase material. When you paraphrase material, follow these steps:

1. Read the information through at least once.
2. Write down keywords to help you remember what you have read, including key statistical information.
3. Without looking at the original source, and using the keywords as a guide, in your own words, write the gist of what you just read. You do not need to write down everything, and you should not do so. Just write the highlights and the important points that relate to your topic.

It is important that you do not look at the original source when you paraphrase the material; if you do, you will probably inadvertently use the original author's words and sentence structure.

Note! Remember that you must include citations when you paraphrase.

Note! You need to include only the information that is relevant to your topic. For example, if you are writing a paper about boys who violate curfew laws, and the original source also includes information about boys who are truant, you do not need to include the information about the boys who are truant.

See **Plagiarism, Class Exercise #4: "Paraphrasing a Paragraph From a Research Report"** at the end of this unit.

NOTES

Plagiarism, Class Exercise #1

Identifying Plagiarism, Part I

Read the following paragraph. Then state all *of the reasons why each example constitutes plagiarism.*

Original Source

"In a study of 2,173 teens who reported being the victim of cyber, physical, psychological, or sexual dating abuse, only 8.6% reported seeking help from at least one person; more females (11%) sought help than males (5.7%). Very few teens—only 4.1% of females and 2% of males—sought help after they experienced dating abuse for the first time" (Oudekerk, Blachman-Demner, & Mulford, 2014, p. 5).

1. In a study of 2,173 teens who reported being the victim of cyber, physical, psychological, or sexual dating abuse, only 8.6% reported seeking help from at least one person; more females (11%) sought help than males (5.7%).

   _____
   _____

2. In a study of 2,173 teens who reported being the victim of cyber, physical, psychological, or sexual dating abuse, only 8.6% reported seeking help from at least one person; more females (11%) sought help than males (5.7%) (Oudekerk, Blachman-Demner, & Mulford, 2014).

   _____
   _____

3. "In a study of 2,173 teens who reported being the victim of cyber, physical, psychological, or sexual dating abuse, only 8.6% reported seeking help from at least one person; more females (11%) sought help than males (5.7%)" (Oudekerk, Blachman-Demner, & Mulford, 2014).

   _____
   _____

4. According to a study of 2,000 teens who reported being the victim of cyber, physical, psychological, or sexual dating abuse, more females sought help than did males. Very few teens sought help after they were abused for the first time.

   _____
   _____

Plagiarism, Class Exercise #1

5. Female teenagers who are first-time victims of dating abuse and those who were abused more frequently are both more likely to ask for help than do male teenagers who were victims of such abuse (Oudekerk, Blachman-Demner, & Mulford, 2014).

_____

_____

_____

Plagiarism, Class Exercise #2

Identifying Plagiarism, Part II

Read the following paragraphs. The first paragraph is a direct quote from a research report. The next four paragraphs are "rewrites" of the first paragraph. For each paragraph, state whether it constitutes plagiarism. Then state all *of the reasons for your answer.*

Original Source

"Most experts agree that any successful violence intervention program must be collaborative. Such programs should also target youth early, before frequent exposure to violence leads them to adopt negative and dysfunctional patterns of behavior" (Office for Victims of Crime [OVC], 2003, p. 1).

1. Experts agree that in order for a violence intervention program to be successful, it must involve several agencies. They also agree that those programs must focus on youth when they are young, before they are exposed to violence that might cause them to engage in bad behaviors (OVC, 2003).

2. According to experts, children who witness violence are more likely to benefit from violence intervention programs if they are participants when they are young (OVC, 2003).

3. Most experts are in agreement that several agencies must work together to create a successful violence intervention program (OVC, 2003). They also agree that such programs should involve youth early, before constant exposure to violence causes them to engage in nonpositive behaviors (OVC, 2003).

4. "Most experts agree that any successful violence intervention program must be collaborative. Such programs should also target youth early, before frequent exposure to violence leads them to adopt negative and dysfunctional patterns of behavior" (OVC, 2003).

Plagiarism, Class Exercise #3

Rewriting Statistics

Using the spaces in the cells of the table, rewrite the following statistical information.

Alternative Ways to Write Statistics				
ORIGINAL	**ALTERNATIVE #1**	**ALTERNATIVE #2**	**ALTERNATIVE #3**	**ALTERNATIVE #4 (OPPOSITE)**
8%	0.08	8/100 (8 out of 100) or 4/50 or 2/25	Almost 10%	92% do (or do not)
3/4				
0.52				
Sample size: 25 males 75 females				

Comparisons

Using the information in the first table, rewrite the statistical information in the blank cells in the second table, comparing the percentages of males versus females who report physical *abuse. Then rewrite the information comparing the percentages reporting* sexual *abuse.*

Percentage Reporting Different Types of Childhood Abuse		
	MALES	**FEMALES**
Physical abuse	23.1	11.6
Sexual abuse	8.7	33.9
Reported Incidents of Childhood Abuse				
	ALTERNATIVE #1	**ALTERNATIVE #2**	**ALTERNATIVE #3**	**ALTERNATIVE #4**
Physical abuse: males vs. females				
Sexual abuse: males vs. females				

Plagiarism, Class Exercise #4

Paraphrasing a Paragraph from a Research Report

For this exercise, assume that your research question is whether today's adolescents experience more incidents of cyber bullying in intimate relationships than incidents of physical, sexual, or psychological abuse. Then read the following information. Using the techniques you learned in class, paraphrase the information and then write a paragraph using the information you have paraphrased. Remember to include the relevant statistical information in your answer.

The following information is from Zweig, J. M., Dank, M., Lachman, P., & Yahner, J. (2013, July). *Technology, teen dating violence and abuse, and bullying.* Retrieved from: www.nij.gov/publications/pages/publication-detail.aspx?ncjnumber=243296

One NIJ-funded study examined the prevalence of dating violence among 5,647 teens (51.8% female, 74.6% Caucasian) from 10 middle schools and high schools (representing Grades 7–12) throughout New York, New Jersey, and Pennsylvania. Findings indicated that within the past year,

- 18.0% of respondents reported experiencing cyber dating abuse (e.g., "My partner used my social networking account without permission" or "My partner sent texts/emails to engage in sexual acts I did not want").
- 20.7% experienced physical dating violence (e.g., reporting that a partner "pushed" or "kicked" the respondent).
- 32.6% experienced psychological dating abuse (e.g., "My partner threatened to hurt me" or "My partner would not let me do things with other people").
- 9.0% experienced sexual coercion (e.g., "My partner pressured me to have sex when [he or she] knew I didn't want to").

The study also specifically examined dating violence rates among teens who had dated within the past year (66% of total teens; $n = 3,745$). The following percentages of dating teens reported experiencing forms of abuse:

- Cyber dating abuse: 26.3%
- Physical dating violence: 29.9%
- Psychological dating abuse: 47.2%
- Sexual coercion: 13.0%

Plagiarism, Handout #1

Rules of Plagiarism Reference Guide

Rule #1: You must cite everything that is not common knowledge.
If it is not common knowledge, you must cite the information.

Rule #2: Do not just write your own thoughts.
All of the information in your paper must come from the sources you read. You must cite those sources.

Rule #3: You must properly paraphrase the material.
Paraphrase means completely changing what you have read.

Rule #4: Follow the list of what *not* to do.
- Do not paraphrase one sentence at a time.
- Do not just change a few words.
- Do not just change the sentence structure.
- Do not just use synonyms.
- Do not just change the order of the sentences or just leave out words.

Doing any of the above and putting a citation at the end is plagiarism.

Rule #5: Include all of the required elements for direct quotes.
- You must use quotation marks (unless it's a block quote, 40+ words),
- You must include a citation at the end of the quote, and
- You must include a page number.

Use a direct quote only if it is said so spectacularly that you cannot paraphrase it.

BOTTOM LINE: IF IN DOUBT, CITE.

Organizing a Paper: From Taking Notes to Creating an Outline

UNIT 4

UNIT SUMMARY
    Learning Objectives
    Organizing an Academic Paper: An Overview
    Taking Notes
        Taking Notes for the Informative Section of a Paper
        Taking Notes for the Persuasive Section of a Paper
    Creating an Outline
        General Format of an Outline
        Creating an Outline from the Notes
            General Rules
            The First Draft
            The Subsequent Drafts
                Major Points
                Minor Points
                The Overall Organization

Learning Objectives

At the end of this unit, students will be able to do the following:

- Effectively take notes from journal articles and research reports.
- Use those notes to create a final outline for a paper.

Organizing an Academic Paper: An Overview

One of the most difficult parts of writing a paper is organizing the material. This is especially true when you have a large amount of information to read. However, if you organize the material as you read through each article, you will get a head start on organizing your paper.

One type of paper you may be asked to write as a criminal justice student is a research paper in which you must discuss the effectiveness of a program or policy. This is sometimes called a policy paper. We will focus on how to organize a policy paper in this unit.

Typically, a policy paper will have two parts. In the first part of the paper, you will educate your reader about your topic. This is called the "informative section." In the second part of the paper, you will discuss studies that have evaluated your program or policy. This is called the "persuasive section." In this unit, you will learn how to take notes for each part of the paper.

 Although most academic papers will have an informative section and a persuasive section, your instructor might assign a paper that does not have both parts, such as an analytical paper. In that case, complete the steps required to take notes only for that particular type of paper.

Taking Notes

There are certain steps you should follow to organize your information as you read through it. The first of these is to take notes for the informative part of your paper.

Taking Notes for the Informative Section of a Paper

Follow these steps when you take notes for the informative section of a paper:

1. On a piece of paper, list the topics the assignment requires you to discuss. Your instructor will provide you with a list of those topics. However, typically, when you write a policy paper, topics you discuss will include a description of the policy or program, the scope of the problem it is trying to address, its history, its purpose or goal, the population targeted, and its elements or activities.

2. Read the first article. As you read it and find the relevant information, highlight it but do not stop to take any notes.

3. After you have read the article, open a blank Word document. At the top, type in the last name(s) of the author(s), the year of publication, and the article's title. Also, give your source a number and type it at the top of the page. You will use that number to identify the article when you take notes.

4. Reread the article carefully, but this time as you read, take notes about the information you must include in your paper. Before each entry, type the topic you are addressing (e.g., history). After each entry, include the number you have assigned to that source and the page number where you found the information. By writing this information, you will be able to

refer back to the page where you found it in the article if you need to. Also, you will use the information about each entry later when you copy and paste it into your final notes page.

Example:

The first source you will take notes on is by Wilson and Carlie. You have labeled this source "source #1."

Wilson & Carlie (2015) "Mental Health Courts"—source #1

History—First program created in FL in 1985 (1, p. 122)

History—Currently, 250 similar programs nationwide (1, p. 124)

Purpose—To offer mentally ill offenders treatment rather than punishment and to reduce recidivism (1, p. 133)

5. After you have taken notes on your first article, follow the same rules for each remaining article, beginning a new Word document for each one. That is, for each article, open a new Word document, write the name(s) of the author(s), year of publication, and the title of the article at the top and assign a number to that source. Then read the article and note the important information in it along with the topic it relates to, the number you assigned to it, and the page number where you found it.
6. After you have finished reading all of your sources and taken notes on all of the information, open a final Word document. Go back through each of the previous documents, and copy and paste all of the information for the first topic into the final document.

Note! Copy and paste the material rather than cutting and pasting it so that you have the information on your original notes pages to refer back to if necessary.

Example:

On your notes page for the article written by Wilson and Carlie (source #1), copy all of the History information, including the parenthetical information (source number and page number) and paste it into your final document. Then go to the notes you have written for source #2, copy all of the History information from it, and move it to your final document under the Wilson and Carlie History entries. Continue to do this for all of the History sections of your notes. When you are finished with this step, you will have all of the History information from each article placed together in your final document.

7. After you have copied and pasted all of the information for your first topic into the final notes page, go back through your notes pages and copy and paste all of the information you have taken from the articles for your second topic (e.g., purpose or goal). Follow these same steps for all of the topics you have included.
8. When you have finished copying and pasting the information from each of the articles, most of the information you will need to write your paper will be in your final document. Moreover, all of the information for each topic you must discuss will be grouped together in your final document. You will copy and paste that information into the appropriate sections of your outline.

Warning! When you take notes, you must completely paraphrase the information. Failing to completely paraphrase the information is plagiarism! If you do not have time to paraphrase as you take notes, put quotation marks around the information you have copied and write a large note to yourself that it is a direct quote. This will help remind you to paraphrase the material before you use it in your paper.

Taking Notes for the Persuasive Section of a Paper

When you take notes for a persuasive section of a paper, you will take notes on the studies that you will discuss. Taking notes for this section of your paper is very similar to taking notes for the informative section of a paper; however, you will not combine the information from the articles as you did previously. Instead, you will take notes for each study and then use those notes to write separate discussions about each study.

To take notes for this part of your paper, follow these steps:

1. On a piece of paper, list the topics your instructor requires you to discuss for each study. When you write a policy paper, these topics typically include the research question, the population examined, how the data were obtained, the findings, and the limitations.
2. Read the first article. As you read it and find the relevant information, highlight it but do not stop to take any notes.
3. After you have read the article, open a blank Word document. At the top, type in the last name(s) of the author(s), the year of publication, and the article's title. You do not have to give the article a number.
4. Reread the article carefully. This time through, write notes about the information you must include in your paper. As you read through the article, write down the information relating to each topic as you find it. Before each entry, write the topic you are addressing (e.g., data obtained, findings). After each entry, write the page number where you found the information. By writing this information, you will be able to refer to the page where you found it, if you need to. In part, your notes page will look like this:

Example:

Wilson & Carlie (2015) "Mental Health Courts"

Research Question—Gender differences in recidivism rates among mental health court participants (p. 121)

Data obtained—Sample of 60 male and 40 female program participants (p. 122)

Data obtained—Interview and arrest records of 60 male and 40 female program participants (p. 122)

Findings—Men more likely to recidivate than women (p. 130)

Findings—Men ages 18–21 most likely to recidivate within the first year (p. 131)

Findings—Women ages 18–21 least likely to recidivate within the first year (p. 131)

When you take notes on the findings of a study, remember that you are only interested in that part of the study that addresses your thesis statement. You do not have to take notes on irrelevant information.

Note! Often, researchers will discuss one topic (e.g., findings) before discussing the next topic (e.g., conclusions). However, some researchers intersperse the topics (e.g., discuss findings with conclusions or limitations). Be careful to write the correct topic before each entry.

After you have taken notes on all of the topics you must address in the first study, open a blank Word document. Type the title of the first study article at the top, together with the last name(s) of the author(s) and the year of publication. Then copy and paste the information so that all of the information about each topic is grouped together. For example, all of your information about Topic 1 will be together, and your information about Topic 2 will be together. You will copy and paste that information into the appropriate section of your outline.

After you have copied and pasted the information for your first study, go back and repeat the steps for your second and third studies. When you are finished, you should have a separate document for each study.

Creating an Outline

The next step in organizing your paper is to use your notes to write an outline. The purpose of writing an outline is to further evaluate and better organize the information you have written in your notes. When you write a paper that has both an informative section and a persuasive section, the first part of your outline will include information for the informative section. The second part of the outline will include information for your persuasive section.

In general, an outline serves as a road map for writing your paper. The more specific and detailed your outline, the easier it will be to write your paper. Moreover, the more detailed your outline, the easier it will be for you to stay on track and not get deterred by side issues.

General Format of an Outline

An outline has major points (major headings) and supporting points (minor headings). In an outline, major headings are denoted by Roman numerals. Minor headings are denoted by capital letters and are used to support the major headings.

Supporting points for minor headings are denoted as numbers. Supporting points for those headings are denoted by lowercase letters. If you use supporting points, you must always have a minimum of two (e.g., at least an "A" and "B," a "1" and "2," an "a" and "b"). Do not write one without the other.

Example:

Write a sample outline using "I," "A," "B," "1," "2," "a," and "b."

_____
_____
_____
_____
_____
_____
_____

Creating an Outline from the Notes

General Rules

When you write your outline, follow these rules:

- Include the source number and page number where you found the information for each supporting point. That will enable you to easily refer back to the original source if you need to. For your studies, you need to include only the page number.
- Write the outline entries as short phrases; do not write complete sentences. In general, each entry should not be longer than one line.

> **Exception!** The entries for your studies may be longer because they will contain more specific information. However, they should still be only one or two lines long.

- You must include an introduction and conclusion in your outline. Thus, Roman numeral I will be your introduction, and the final Roman numeral will be your conclusion.

The First Draft

When you write an outline, begin with your major points (denoted by Roman numerals) for the informative section. These constitute the main ideas for that part of your paper. The major points are the elements required by your assignment. You should list them in the same order that they are listed in your assignment. For example, Roman numeral II will be "Topic 1," Roman numeral III will be "Topic 2," and Roman numeral IV will be "Topic 3."

After you have listed your major points, list your minor points. To do this, go back to your notes and copy and paste all of the information (including the source and page numbers) for the first topic you must discuss. Because you should only use short phrases in an outline, you may need to rewrite the information into short phrases.

After you have copied and pasted the information about that topic, you will need to organize it in your outline.

Example:

One of your sections is "History." For that section, you have copied and pasted information stating, "First program began in 1985 (source #, p. #), started in FL (source #, p. #), currently, more than 250 programs in the U.S. (source #, p. #)." Each piece of information will become a minor point in your outline as follows:

III. History of mental health courts
    A. Began in 1985 (source #, p. #)
    B. Started in FL (source #, p. #)
    C. Currently, 250 similar programs nationwide (source #, p. #)

After you have copied, pasted, and organized the minor points for the first major point, repeat the process for each of the other major points.

Creating an Outline

The next part of your outline includes the notes that you have taken for the persuasive section of your paper. The major points that you should include in your outline are the studies that have evaluated your program or policy. To create the minor points for those sections of your outline, follow the same steps that you used to create the minor points for the informative section. Specifically, for the first study, go back to your notes and copy and paste all of the information (including page numbers) for the first point (Topic 1). Again, because you should only use short phrases in an outline, you may need to rewrite the information. After you have copied and pasted the information for the first point, repeat the process for each of the other points.

> **Example:**
>
> One of your topics is the researchers' findings. For your first study, you have copied and pasted information stating, "Men more likely to recidivate than women (p. #), men ages 18 to 21 most likely to recidivate within the first year (p. #), women ages 18 to 21 least likely to recidivate within the first year (p. #)." Because you have more than one finding, you must create a minor point called "Findings" and then list each of those findings as supporting points.
>
> VII. Study #1—Wilson & Carlie (2015)
> A. Research question—Gender differences in recidivism rates among mental health court participants (p. #)
> B. Data—Interviews and arrest records of 60 male and 40 female program participants (p. #)
> C. Findings
>   1. Men more likely to recidivate than women (p. #)
>   2. Men ages 18–21 most likely to recidivate within the first year (p. #)
>   3. Women ages 18–21 least likely to recidivate within the first year (p. #)

The Subsequent Drafts

After you have written your first draft, you must revise it. When you do the revision, concentrate on the major points, the minor points, and the overall organization of the information.

Major Points

As you read and revise your outline, consider these questions about your major points (Roman numerals):

- Do any of the major points contain so many supporting points that it would be better to split them into two or more major points?

> **Example:**
>
> "Purpose and goals" is one of your major points. Look at how much information you have for each topic. If you find that you have a great deal, it may be better to split those topics and write them as two major points in your outline. Doing this will improve the readability and organization of your paper.

- Do any of the major points contain information either that is not very important or that should be included instead as a supporting point for another topic?

> **Example:**
>
> One of the topics you discuss in your paper is the population that the program is designed to help. If you have listed each of the characteristics of the population as major points, you should rewrite them as minor points under the major point "Population served."

- Did you include as major points all of the topics your assignment requires you to discuss for both the informative and persuasive sections of your paper, including the topics required for each of the studies? If you have not, you need to add the missing information to your outline.

Minor Points

After you have looked at your major points in your outline, look at the contents of your minor points. Consider these questions about your minor points:

- Would it make your paper stronger if you included the information as a major point, rather than as a minor point?

> **Example:**
>
> You have included "Purpose" as a supporting point for "Goals." Because these are both important points, and both have supporting information, rewrite "Purpose" as a major point in your outline.

- Are your supporting points detailed enough, or have you left out important information?

> **Example:**
>
> You are writing a paper about drunk drivers. One of your major points is the definition of drunk drivers. You have listed gender and age as minor points. However, the literature also discusses legal limits and ethnic groups. In your outline, you should add those two minor points. In addition, determine whether there are any supporting points for those minor points (e.g., for gender, you can list the supporting points "Male" and "Female").

- For sections in which you discuss the studies, did you include as minor points all of the information your assignment requires?

> **Example:**
>
> The assignment requires that you discuss specific information about the studies, including the sample population, how the data were obtained, the researcher's findings, and any limitations. If you have omitted any of that information, you must add it to your outline.

Creating an Outline

The Overall Organization

After you have looked at the content of the major and minor points of your outline, look at the overall organization of your information. When you create your outline, you must write it so that the material makes sense, flows well, and is in a logical order.

Hint! The best way to ensure that your paper is well organized is to discuss the elements in the same order in which your instructor listed them in the assignment.

Beware! Making sure that your outline is "detailed" means using many headings and subheadings. It does not mean writing long explanations for each entry.

*See **Organizing a Paper, Handout #1: "Sample Outline"** at the end of this unit.*

*See **Organizing a Paper, Take-Home Assignment #1: "Drafting an Outline"** at the end of this unit.*

NOTES

Organizing a Paper, Handout #1

Sample Outline

Thesis statement: *Drunk drivers are less likely to recidivate if they receive punishment rather than treatment.*

 If you are writing an analytical paper, you will not have a thesis statement, but you will have to include a research question.

I. Introduction
   A. Statistics on prevalence of drunk driving in the United States (source #, p. #)
   B. Costs associated with drunk driving (source #, p. #)
   C. Two approaches to reducing drunk driving (source #, p. #)
      1. Punishment (source #, p. #)
      2. Rehabilitation (source #, p. #)
   D. Thesis statement (source #, p. #)

II. Scope of the problem
   A. Summary of most recent estimates of number of drunk driving incidents in the United States (source #, p. #)
   B. Summary of most recent estimates of drunk driving fatalities in the United States (source #, p. #)

III. Define drunk drivers
   A. Legal limits (source #, p. #)
      1. DUI—Minimum blood alcohol content 0.08 (source #, p. #)
      2. DWI—Minimum blood alcohol content 0.07 (source #, p. #)
   B. Prevalence—Offender demographics
      1. Gender (source #, p. #)
         a. Male (source #, p. #)
         b. Female (source #, p. #)
      2. Ethnic groups (source #, p. #)
         a. Caucasian (source #, p. #)
         b. African American (source #, p. #)
         c. Hispanic (source #, p. #)
      3. Age (source #, p. #)
         a. Legal age (21 and over) (source #, p. #)
         b. Under age (under 21) (source #, p. #)

IV. History of DUI legislation
   A. First legislation passed in 1910 (source #, p. #)
   B. California first state with legislation against drunk driving (source #, p. #)
   C. Many states had passed laws by the 1990s (source #, p. #)
   D. Currently, all states have laws against drunk driving (source #, p. #)

Organizing a Paper, Handout #1

V. Punishment
   A. Confinement (source #, p. #)
      1. Prison (source #, p. #)
      2. Home detention (source #, p. #)
   B. Fines (source #, p. #)
   C. Removal of privileges (source #, p. #)
      1. Take away driver's license (source #, p. #)
      2. Take away license plates (source #, p. #)
      3. Ignition interlock devices (source #, p. #)

VI. Treatment programs
   A. In-patient (source #, p. #)
      1. Alcohol-related programs (source #, p. #)
      2. Mental health therapy (source #, p. #)
   B. Outpatient (source #, p. #)
      1. Alcohol-related programs (source #, p. #)
         a. Alcoholics Anonymous (source #, p. #)
         b. Alcohol education classes (source #, p. #)
      2. Mental health therapy (source #, p. #)

VII. Study #1—Smith & Jones, 2015
   A. Do ignition interlock devices reduce recidivism for first-time DUI offenders? (Research question) (p. #)
   B. 350 convicted DUI offenders in NM from 2005 to 2010 (Sample population) (p. #)
   C. Data obtained from interviews, questionnaires (Data obtained) (p. #)
   D. 55% of sample population did not recidivate after 1 year (Findings) (p. #)
   E. Small sample size may affect findings (Limitations) (p. #)

VIII. Study #2—Wells, 2014
   A. Are repeat DUI offenders who receive 1–3 years in prison less likely to recidivate? (p. #)
   B. 1,500 offenders, nationwide, examined in 2010 (p. #)
   C. Data obtained from interviews, questionnaires (p. #)
   D. 51% of those offenders did not recidivate (p. #)
   E. Problems with data collection may have skewed results (p. #)

IX. Study #3—Wilson, 2015
   A. Does the combined punishment of imposing a fine and revoking a DUI offender's driver's license reduce likelihood that offender will drink and drive in the future? (p. #)
   B. 4,000 offenders from three Midwest states (p. #)
   C. Data obtained from self-report surveys, interviews (p. #)
   D. Offenders who received combination of punishments less likely to drink and drive; however, if they received only one, not less likely to drink and drive (p. #)
   E. Self-report survey may have led to underreporting, inaccurate answers (p. #)

Organizing a Paper, Handout #1

X. Conclusion
  A. Summary statement of problem and impact on society (source #, p. #)
  B. Restate thesis statement
  C. Future implications (source #, p. #)
    1. Create more ways to educate people about drunk driving and the repercussions for committing it (source #, p. #)
    2. Conduct more studies examining combination of punishment and treatment to reduce recidivism (source #, p. #)

Organizing a Paper, Take-Home Assignment #1

Creating an Outline

1. At the top of the page, write your thesis statement.
2. Create a detailed outline of your paper, which lays out a summary of the information you will present in your final paper. The outline must include the minimum number of section heads and subtopics required by your instructor. The outline also must follow the format taught in this unit (e.g., use of Roman numerals, capital letters).

Clue! To create your main section heads, refer to the description of the required content for your paper as provided by your instructor.

3. For each *subsection head* in your outline, write the last name(s) of the author(s) and year of publication of the article(s) that you are relying on to create those subsections.
4. Submit abstracts of all of the sources you will be using to write your paper.

Mechanics of Writing: From the First Draft to the Final Paper

UNIT 5

UNIT SUMMARY
  Learning Objectives
  Academic Writing: An Introduction
  Writing an Academic Paper: General Rules
  Writing an Academic Paper: From the First Draft to the Final Draft
    Getting Started: Writing the First Draft
    Writing and Editing the Second (and Subsequent) Drafts
      Writing and Editing a Paper on a Global Level
        The Introduction
        The Discussion
        The Conclusion
      Writing and Editing a Paper on a Local Level
      Specific Mechanical and Grammatical Rules to Follow
        Sentence Structure and Content Rules
        Grammar Rules
        Punctuation Rules
        Rules About Numbers
        Rules About Gender
        Race and Ethnicity Rules
      Commonly Confused Words
  Assembling Your Final Paper: From the Title Page to the Reference List
    Creating a Title Page
    Creating a Running Head With Page Numbers
    Attaching the Reference List
  Proofreading Your Paper: The Final Step
    Proofreading: General Rules
    Proofreading Your Paper: A Checklist

Unit 5 | Mechanics of Writing: From the First Draft to the Final Paper

Learning Objectives

At the end of this unit, students will be able to do the following:

- Differentiate between academic writing and other less-formal styles of writing.
- Write and edit an academic paper using proper grammar, sentence structure, topic sentences, and transitions.
- Identify common grammatical and mechanical errors.
- Properly proofread a paper.

Academic Writing: An Introduction

Academic writing is a formal writing style. There are some basic rules for writing in a formal style, which you will learn about in more detail later. However, here are a few general rules to help you understand what formal writing entails.

1. Do not use slang or informal terminology.

Example:

Improper (informal): Cops
Proper (formal): Police officers, law enforcement officers

Example:

Improper (informal): Teens, kids
List five proper (formal) words that you could use instead of *teens* or *kids*.
_____
_____

2. Write objectively. Do not put yourself in the paper by using first person terminology such as "I," "my," "we," "us," or "our." Also, do not include personal opinions in your paper.
3. Write concisely. Say what you need to say in as few words as possible; use simple rather than complex sentences.
4. Do not attempt to impress the reader by using grandiose language. It is easier to read and understand writing that is straightforward and to the point.
5. Write as you speak (but without the slang).
6. Do not editorialize (i.e., do not preface facts or statistics with an adverb; simply state the statistic).

Example:

Improper: Tragically, 5% of all children are assaulted at some point in their lives.
Rewrite the sentence without editorializing.
_____

Writing an Academic Paper: From the First Draft to the Final Draft 93

7. Do not overstate or exaggerate a fact.

> **Example:**
> *Improper:* It is absolutely imperative that the study be conducted.
> Rewrite the sentence so that it does not exaggerate a fact.
> _____

8. Do not use flowery or creative language. That is acceptable in creative writing, but it is not acceptable in a formal academic paper.
9. Avoid jargon (technical vocabulary or specialized words used in a profession); instead, use words and phrases more commonly used in the field. The best way to become familiar with the most common words and phrases is to read research articles and reports.

> See **Mechanics of Writing, Class Exercise #1: "Identifying Mechanical Errors"** at the end of this unit.

Writing an Academic Paper: General Rules

When you write a paper, you should follow these rules:

1. Type your paper double-spaced, using a 12-point Arial, Times New Roman, or Helvetica font, unless your instructor tells you otherwise. Use the margins that your word processing program defaults to; do not set them to accommodate the amount of material you have (too much or too little). Do not add extra line breaks between paragraphs by pressing ENTER twice.
2. Write your paper in essay format. This means you must use full sentences and correct grammar and spelling.
3. Save your paper to your computer frequently as you work on it. At the end of each session, save your paper to an external source such as a flash drive or "the cloud," or print out what you have written; that way, if you have problems with your computer, you will always have a backup copy of your paper.
4. Each time you save your paper, rename it (e.g., "version 1," "version 2"). This allows you to easily find the latest version of your work and to refer back to an earlier version if you need to.
5. Use spell check as you write your paper, but remember that it will not catch some errors (e.g., if you mistakenly type "there" instead of "their," or if you inadvertently type the wrong word [e.g., you type "sit" instead of "hit"]).
6. Use grammar checker with caution. It will often make incorrect suggestions.

Writing an Academic Paper: From the First Draft to the Final Draft

Writing a paper is a process; you should write many drafts before you hand in the final one. Typically, the first draft you write will be very rough. With each subsequent draft, your paper will begin to look more like a finished product.

Getting Started: Writing the First Draft

Often, the most difficult part of writing a paper is getting started. To overcome this hurdle, follow these general rules:

1. Prepare an outline. You will use the outline as a road map to guide you as you write. It will also ensure that your paper is well-organized.
2. The first time you sit down to work on your paper, just write. Do not worry about correct spelling or punctuation, or how your words sound. Just write what you want to say.
3. Do not stop and edit each sentence. Not only will you get lost in the details, but paying close attention to the little things at this stage can often lead to a discouraging lack of progress. You will go back and fix the errors in later drafts.

Writing and Editing the Second (and Subsequent) Drafts

Once you have written the gist of what you want to include in your first draft, you will go back through your paper and begin to edit it. With your second and subsequent drafts, you will read your paper with a critical eye and pay attention to the details of what you have written. Because you will need to concentrate on many details, we will discuss each of them separately.

Writing and Editing a Paper on a Global Level

You should first concentrate on the global (overall) organization of your paper. You should have an introduction, a discussion, and a conclusion. Using your outline as a guide, and the information you have written so far, start refining those elements.

The Introduction The introduction is a short preview of your paper. Its purpose is to let the reader know what your paper will be about. If you are writing an argumentative paper, you must include your thesis statement in your introduction. If you are writing an analytical paper, you must include your research question in your introduction.

When you write your introduction, make it interesting. The more interesting your introduction is, the more likely the reader will want to continue reading. There are several ways to make your introduction interesting:

- Think of your introduction as being similar to a movie trailer. You want to catch your readers' attention and convince them that the paper is worth reading. One way to do this is to include a relevant statistic describing the scope of the problem you are addressing.

> **Example:**
>
> You are writing a paper about the benefits of drug courts. One of the arguments you will make in favor of the courts is that they help to reduce the caseloads of overburdened criminal court systems. Sample sentences for your introduction might be:
>
> *According to Rosenmerkel, Durose, and Farole (2009), in 2006, approximately 1.1 million people were convicted of a felony in state courts. Of that number, approximately 33% of the convictions were for a drug offense.*
>
> You could then go on to explain that, in response, jurisdictions created drug courts to help ease the courts' caseloads. By including specific statistics, you make your introduction more interesting and give your reader a reason to want to continue reading the paper.

Writing an Academic Paper: From the First Draft to the Final Draft

- Present a recent relevant media story in your introduction. By giving readers a real-world example to support your position, you pique their interest in your topic, encouraging them to read more. If you use this technique, include some background information or a brief history about your topic so that your readers better understand why you are using that example.

> **Example:**
> You are writing a paper about the death penalty. In it, you will argue that it should be abolished because of the number of people who have been wrongfully convicted and executed. To support your contention, you will discuss the use of DNA evidence to exonerate inmates sentenced to death. A sample introduction might read:
>
> In the United States, the use of the death penalty has been controversial for many years. On the one hand, supporters contend that it should not be abolished because it serves as a deterrent to committing crimes. On the other hand, opponents of the death penalty argue that it should be abolished because many people have been wrongfully convicted and executed. In fact, recently, the media reported about a man who has been exonerated by DNA evidence after spending 30 years in prison for sexual assault (Carlton, 2011). Moreover, it was reported that since 2001, 41 convicted offenders have been released from Texas prisons after being exonerated by DNA evidence (Carlton, 2011). To save other innocent people from being wrongfully executed, the death penalty should be abolished.

Note! In the preceding example, the last sentence in the introduction is the thesis statement for the paper.

Warning! An introduction is a *short* preview; therefore, it should be no longer than three-quarters of a page. If your introduction is longer than that, review it to see if you have included unnecessary information.

The Discussion The discussion (or body) follows the introduction and is the meat of your paper. Proper organization of the discussion is very important, so be sure to follow your outline. Because you are a criminal justice student, your instructor may require you to write a paper about a program or policy and discuss what researchers have found about its effectiveness. Therefore, in this section, we will discuss what you should include in this section of a policy paper.

When you write the discussion section of a policy paper, you must assume that your readers have little to no knowledge about the program or policy you will discuss. As such, you must first educate them. To do this, include a brief discussion about the nature and scope of the problem that led to the creation of the program or policy, a description of the program or policy, a discussion of its elements, and a discussion of its purposes or goals.

For example, assume you are writing a paper about the benefits of drug courts. Your first step is to discuss the nature and scope of the problem that led to the creation of these courts.

> **Example:**
>
> At this point in your paper, you could discuss the problem of drug abuse in the United States and the high numbers of arrests and convictions for drug-related offenses. You could then discuss how those convictions have resulted in an increase in the number of people incarcerated for those offenses and, in turn, prison overcrowding. Finally, you could write that one of the reasons drug courts were created was to address the issues associated with prison overcrowding. Other relevant information you could include here are the dates the courts were first created and how many courts currently exist in the United States.

Once you have discussed the nature and scope of the problem leading to the creation of drug courts, explain to your reader what a drug court is.

> **Example:**
>
> In this part of the paper, you could discuss elements of drug courts. These may include such things as which offenders are eligible to participate, which professionals are involved (e.g., judges, attorneys, drug counselors), and what role each person plays in relation to the offender. You could also discuss what offenders must do to successfully complete the drug court requirements.

Your final step in educating your reader is to discuss the goals (or purposes) of drug courts.

> **Example:**
>
> In this part of the paper, you could explain that two goals of drug courts are to reduce recidivism and to help the offender become drug free. You would then discuss how the courts help offenders achieve those goals.

Now your readers have a basic understanding about the problem(s) leading to the creation of the program or policy and about the program or policy itself. This knowledge will help your readers better understand the rest of your paper, which will include a discussion about studies that have been conducted to examine the success of the program or policy.

The Conclusion The conclusion is a brief summary of the important points of your paper. You should not reiterate everything you have written, nor should you include new information. If you are writing an argumentative paper, you should restate your thesis statement in the conclusion. If you are writing an analytical paper, you should answer your research question in the conclusion.

If relevant, you should also suggest a course of action for the research to follow. For example, if more research needs to be conducted on certain issues pertaining to your topic, you should state that.

> **Warning!** As with the introduction, the conclusion is a *brief* summary. If your conclusion is longer than three-quarters of a page, review it to see if you have included unnecessary information.

Writing an Academic Paper: From the First Draft to the Final Draft   97

Writing and Editing a Paper on a Local Level

After you have looked at your paper on a global level, you must concentrate specifically on the paragraphs and sentences. This is also known as editing on a local level. When you edit on a local level, follow these general rules:

1. Include only one idea per paragraph. For example, as you write about topic A, do not go off on a tangent about topic B and then return to topic A. Write *only* about topic A.

> **Example:**
>
> If you are writing a paragraph about the daily activities of a boot camp inmate, do not mention, in the middle of the paragraph, how many boot camps exist in the United States.

To determine whether you have written only one idea, look at each paragraph and, in the margin, write the idea that you are discussing (i.e., if you are discussing the history of your program, write *history*). If you find you have written about more than one idea, revise that paragraph.

2. Do not violate the "clumping rule." When you write, place all similar ideas together in your paper. In other words, you must group together all of your discussions about a particular issue or element. For example, if you are writing a paper about a particular program, all of the discussion about the history of that program must be in one section of your paper. You should not discuss the history on one page and then mention it again several pages later.

To determine whether you have adhered to this rule, write the topic of each paragraph in the margin of your paper. If you find that your discussion about a particular topic appears in several different places in your paper, reorganize your paper so that similar information is discussed in only one place.

3. Begin every paragraph with a topic sentence. This is a very broad statement that tells readers what the paragraph will be about. All of the following sentences in the paragraph must support that topic sentence. In other words, everything you discuss in that paragraph must relate to the topic sentence.

Topic sentences are important because they make it easier for the readers to understand what the paragraph is about and to follow your train of thought. Paragraphs that do not have topic sentences tend to be very difficult to understand.

> **Example:**
>
> In a paragraph in which you discuss the specific daily activities of boot camp inmates, a good topic sentence would be similar to the following:
>
> > Boot camp inmates must participate in certain daily activities.
>
> Your subsequent sentences in that paragraph will discuss only those activities. You will not discuss anything else.

To help you determine whether you have used a topic sentence for every paragraph, and whether each topic sentence is the correct one to use for that paragraph, underline the first sentence of each paragraph. Then ask yourself whether the rest of the sentences in the paragraph support that topic sentence. If they do not, you must either rewrite your topic sentence or rewrite some or all of the remaining sentences in that paragraph.

> See **Mechanics of Writing, Class Exercise #2: "Topic Sentences"** at the end of this unit.

4. Each paragraph must be an acceptable length—neither too long nor too short. You must write at least three sentences in each paragraph; anything shorter than that does not constitute a paragraph. There is no maximum length for a paragraph, but because it should discuss only one idea, most paragraphs tend to be a half page or less.
5. Use transition sentences. These connect one paragraph to the next paragraph and help a paper flow. In addition, they lead the readers from one topic to the next.

Example:

You are writing a paper about the benefits of animals in prison programs. The first paragraph states:

> There are many benefits to animals in prison programs. The first benefit is that they help inmates learn new skills that they can use after they are released from prison. For example, inmates who work with dogs learn how to take care of them by feeding and grooming them. They also learn basic dog-training techniques as well as the best ways to exercise a dog.

A proper transition to the next paragraph sentence would be:

> A second benefit of animals in prison programs is that they help to "better" the inmate. Specifically, inmates who participate in the programs develop an increased sense of self-esteem and become more confident. Moreover, because their work with the dogs will help people with disabilities, the inmates learn compassion for others.

By starting the second paragraph with a transition sentence (which also serves as the topic sentence for the paragraph), the writing flows and readers are able to easily follow the author's train of thought.

6. Use transition words. These connect the sentences within a paragraph. They are important because they help make the sentences flow and the writing less choppy.

> See **Mechanics of Writing, Handout #1: "Transition Words and Phrases"** at the end of this unit.

There are several things you should note about this handout.

- Under the section, "To list items of information or items relating to time," if you use "second . . . third," you must have used "first."

Example:

Rewrite the following sentence so that it is correct:

The inmate had breakfast; second, he cleaned his cell; and third, he went to his job.

_____

_____

Writing an Academic Paper: From the First Draft to the Final Draft   99

- Under the section, "To indicate a difference," if you use "on the one hand," you must follow that with "on the other hand." Similarly, if you use "on the other hand," you must have previously written "on the one hand." In other words, you always must include two hands.

Example:

Rewrite the following sentences so that they are correct:

On the one hand, strict sentencing guidelines punish offenders who have violated the law. However, they may also lead to prison overcrowding.

_____

_____

_____

See **Mechanics of Writing, Class Exercise #3: "Selecting Correct Transition Words"** and **Mechanics of Writing, Handout #2: "Sample Paragraphs"** at the end of this unit.

Specific Mechanical and Grammatical Rules to Follow

Students make many common errors when they write papers. Therefore, you should use the following specific mechanical and grammatical rules when you edit your paper in order to avoid making those mistakes.

Sentence Structure and Content Rules

1. Do not write long (run-on) sentences. Each sentence should include only one idea. Typically, a sentence is too long because it includes too many ideas. If you want to discuss more than one idea, write several sentences, rather than one long one.

   There are two easy ways to help you determine whether a sentence is too long:
   a. Use the "breath rule." Read the sentence out loud. If you have to take a breath, it is too long.
   b. Look at the sentence. If it is longer than two lines, review it. If you have used "and" several times to tie together thoughts, the sentence is probably too long.

2. Write concise, uncomplicated sentences. Say what you need to say in as few words as possible. Do not write long, flowing, or flowery sentences in an attempt to make your paper longer.

Example:

Improper: Due to the fact that the inmate threatened a guard, he was sent to solitary confinement. Rewrite the sentence so it is not wordy.

_____

_____

Example:

Improper: It is absolutely essential to conduct the study.

Rewrite the sentence so it is not wordy.
_____

3. Avoid writing stilted sentences. Vary the length and content of your sentences so that they do not all sound the same.

Example:

Improper: The police officer walked over to the car. The police officer told the driver to put down his window. The police officer asked the driver for his license.

Rewrite the example so that it is not stilted.
_____
_____

4. Do not repeat yourself by using synonyms. You need to say something only once to get your point across.

Example:

Improper: The jury did not understand or comprehend the testimony.

Rewrite the sentence without the unnecessary synonym.
_____

5. Write as you speak (but without the slang).
6. Do not use flowery or grandiose language in an attempt to impress your reader. It is easier to understand straightforward, simple writing, than it is to understand complex writing.

Example:

Improper: The rising of the sun was extraordinarily impressive in its beauty.

Rewrite the sentence without the flowery language.
_____

Writing an Academic Paper: From the First Draft to the Final Draft   101

7. Write objectively; do not put your personal opinions into your paper. For example, do not use "I," "we," "us," or "our."

Example:

Improper: In our society, I think that many youths commit crimes.

Rewrite the sentence so that it is written objectively.
_____

8. Do not editorialize. Say what you need to say without including an introductory adverb that indicates your position.

Example:

Improper: Tragically, many children are abused every day.

Proper: Many children are abused every day.

9. Write in the active rather than passive voice. Sentences that are written in the active voice begin with the person (or thing) who is doing the action. Using the active voice makes your writing stronger and helps the reader understand and follow your thoughts.

Example:

Improper: The prison was overtaken by inmates.

Rewrite the sentence in the active voice.
_____

10. Write your sentences so that you use parallel sentence structure (e.g., between . . . and; neither . . . nor; either . . . or).
11. Do not use contractions. In other words: don't use *don't*.
12. Do not use slashes. Write out "his or her" and "he or she." Do not write "his/her" or "he/she."

Example:

Improper: An inmate is required to keep his/her cell clean.

Rewrite the sentence without the slash.
_____

13. Do not use apostrophes when writing decades and the plurals of numbers.

> **Example:**
>
> *Improper:* In the 1990's, many juveniles were arrested for drunk driving.
> Rewrite the sentence so that it is correct.
> _____
>
> *Improper:* The man who was arrested was in his 60's.
> Rewrite the sentence so that it is correct.
> _____

14. Abbreviate the name of an organization after you have written out the full name. For example, if you are writing an article in which you refer to the Department of Justice, the first time you write the name, write Department of Justice (DOJ). Every subsequent time you refer to it, you can just write DOJ.
15. Remember that the word "data" is plural (the singular is "datum").

> **Example:**
>
> *Improper:* The data was analyzed.
> Rewrite the sentence so that it is correct.
> _____

Grammar Rules

1. Each noun must match its pronoun. If the noun is singular, the pronoun must be singular, too. Similarly, if the noun is plural, the pronoun must be plural.

In the following example, *each student* is singular, so the proper pronouns are *his* or *her*. It is improper to use the pronoun *their*.

> **Example:**
>
> *Improper:* Each student must turn in their paper tonight.
> *Proper:* Each student must turn in his or her paper tonight.

In the following example, *students* is plural, so the correct pronoun to use is *their*, which is also plural.

> **Example:**
>
> *Improper:* The students must hand in his or her papers tonight.
> *Proper:* The students must hand in their papers tonight.

In some situations, the noun is gender specific. If that is the case, you must make sure you use the correct gender for your pronoun.

Writing an Academic Paper: From the First Draft to the Final Draft

Example:

Improper: At the men's detention center, each inmate is required to clean their cell.
Rewrite the sentence so that the pronoun is correct.
_____

2. When you present other people's research, write the findings in the past tense.

Example:

Improper: In his study, Smith (2013) finds that boys are more likely to commit petty crimes than are girls.
Rewrite the sentence so that it is written in the correct verb tense.
_____

3. Use coordinating verb tenses when you list a series of activities (this is called parallelism). For example, if the first two verbs are in the past tense, the final verb must also be in the past tense.

Example:

Improper: The officer saw the suspect, yelled for him to stop, and is chasing him.
Rewrite the sentence so that all of the verb tenses are correct.
_____

Punctuation Rules

1. Place periods and commas inside quotation marks.

Example:

Improper: The judge said, "Order in the court".
Rewrite the sentence so that the punctuation is correct.
_____

2. Place other punctuation marks (i.e., exclamation points and question marks) inside the quotation marks when they are part of the quote. If they are not part of the quote, place them outside the quotation marks.

Example:

Improper: The foreman of the jury stated, "We find the defendant guilty"!
Rewrite the sentence so that the punctuation is correct.
_____

> **Example:**
>
> *Improper:* Did the police officer say, "Drop your weapon?"
> Rewrite the sentence so that the punctuation is correct.
> _____

3. When you list three or more items, separate each element with a comma, including a comma before the final element.

> **Example:**
>
> *Improper:* The study examined physical abuse of men, women and children.
> Rewrite the sentence so that the punctuation is correct.
> _____

Rules About Numbers

1. Write out all numbers less than 10. However, there are several exceptions to this rule.
   a. When you write a percentage, write the number rather than the word. In addition, when you write a percentage with a numeral, use the percent sign, rather than the word *percent*.

> **Example:**
>
> *Improper:* Approximately four percent of children are abused by a relative.
> Rewrite the sentence so that it is correct.
> _____

   b. When you write numbers that refer to ages, write the numbers rather than the words.

> **Example:**
>
> *Improper:* The study included seven-year-olds and eleven-year-olds.
> *Proper:* The study included 7-year-olds and 11-year-olds.
> *Improper:* The study examined youths between the ages of eight and twelve.
> Rewrite the sentence so that it is correct.
> _____

Writing an Academic Paper: From the First Draft to the Final Draft

    c. When you write numbers that state a proportion, write the number rather than the word.

Example:

Improper: Boys are four times more likely than girls to commit a status offense.
Rewrite the sentence so that the number is correct.

_____

2. Certain numbers should always be written as words. These include
   a. numbers that are the first word in a sentence,

Example:

Improper: 15 inmates were involved in the fight.
Rewrite the sentence so that the number is correct.

_____

    b. fractions,

Example:

Improper: Approximately 1/4 of the inmates are women.
Rewrite the sentence so that the number is correct.

_____

    c. and numbers when used in combination with ordinals (numbers that express order, e.g., first, second, third) in a phrase or sentence.

Example:

Improper: Researchers found errors in the first 3 datasets.
Rewrite the sentence so that it is correct.

_____

Rules About Gender

1. Be consistent in the way you use gender terms (i.e., do not write *male* and *woman* together in a sentence; use *men* and *women* or *males* and *females*).

Example:

Improper: More men were arrested than females.
Rewrite the sentence so that it is correct.

_____

2. Use the proper gender terms based on age. In particular, if you are writing about children who are younger than 12 years old, you should refer to them as *boys* and *girls*. If you are writing about teenagers between the ages of 13 and 17, you should refer to them as *male adolescents* and *female adolescents* or as *young men* and *young women*. Finally, if you are writing about people who are 18 and older, you should refer to them as *men* and *women*.

Race and Ethnicity Rules

1. When you write about racial and ethnic groups, the terms are treated as proper nouns and should be capitalized (e.g., Black, White, Asian Americans).
2. When you refer to individuals by racial groups, do not include ethnic groups in your list. In other words, do not describe some individuals by color and others by cultural heritage.

> **Example:**
>
> *Improper:* The sample population included Whites, Blacks, and Asian Americans.
> Rewrite the sentence so that it is correct.
> _____

3. Do not hyphenate multiword racial designations.

> **Example:**
>
> *Improper:* African-American, Native-American
> Rewrite the terms so that they are correct.
> _____

Commonly Confused Words

There are several words that students commonly confuse. During the editing process, if you see any of these words in your paper, stop and ask yourself whether you have chosen the correct word.

1. *Its versus it's.* *It's* always means *it is* or *it has*. *It's* is a contraction, not a possessive pronoun. To determine whether you have used the correct word, when you see *it's*, substitute *it is* or *it has*. If the sentence does not make sense, the correct word to use is *its*.

> **Example:**
>
> *Improper:* The shelter for homeless women lost it's funding.
> Rewrite the sentence so that it is correct.
> _____

2. *Between versus among.* Use the word *between* when you are referring to two people or things. Use the word *among* when you are referring to three or more people or things.

Writing an Academic Paper: From the First Draft to the Final Draft   107

Example:

Improper: There was an altercation among the two gang members.

Rewrite the sentence so that it is correct.

_____

Example:

Improper: The four youths divided the stolen goods between themselves.

Rewrite the sentence so that it is correct.

_____

3. *Number versus amount.* Use the word *number* when you can count individual items or actions (theoretically or in reality). Use the word *amount* when you are referring to a quantity or sum.

Example:

Improper: The amount of arrests last year was higher than the previous year.

Rewrite the sentence so that it is correct.

_____

An example of the proper use of the word *amount* is: "There was a large amount of confusion after someone fired a gun."

4. *Since versus because.* *Since* refers to time. If you are having difficulty remembering which word to use in your sentence, substitute the word *because* for the word *since*. If it makes sense, *because* is the proper word to use.

Example:

Improper: Since the inmate assaulted the guard, he lost all of his privileges.

Rewrite the sentence so that it is correct.

_____

An example of the proper use of the word *since* is "The inmate has been in the detention center since last summer."

5. *i.e. versus e.g.* Both are Latin abbreviations, but they are used in different contexts: *i.e.* means "that is"; therefore, you should use *i.e.* when you want to explain or clarify your point. In contrast, *e.g.* means "for example"; you should use it when you want to strengthen your point by giving an example. When you use *i.e.* or *e.g.* within the context of a sentence, they are parenthetical; that is, you must always follow either abbreviation with a comma, and you must never begin a sentence with these abbreviations.

> **Example:**
>
> *Improper:* The offender was convicted of using a deadly weapon (e.g., a gun).
> *Proper:* The offender was convicted of using a deadly weapon (i.e., a gun).
> *Improper:* Many offenders commit violent crimes (i.e., rape, assault, murder).
> *Proper:* Many offenders commit violent crimes (e.g., rape, assault, murder).

If you are confused about which term to use, substitute *in other words* for *i.e.*; if it makes sense, then *i.e.* is the correct abbreviation to use. If it does not make sense, then *e.g.* is the correct abbreviation to use.

6. *Then versus than.* *Then* refers to time (as in, next in time); *than* is used to make a comparison.

> **Example:**
>
> *Improper:* The lawyer visited his client in jail and than he posted her bond.
> Rewrite the sentence so that it is correct.
> _____
>
> *Improper:* The new jail is larger then the old one.
> Rewrite the sentence so that it is correct.
> _____

7. *That versus who.* Use *that* when referring to anything that is not human. Use *who* when referring to people.

> **Example:**
>
> *Improper:* The man that was convicted of DUI was required to attend a treatment program.
> Rewrite the sentence so that it is correct.
> _____

8. *Their versus they're versus there.* *Their* is possessive (their guns), *they're* is the contraction of *they are*, and *there* refers to a place (over there).
9. *That versus which.* *That* is used with a restrictive clause whereas *which* is used with a nonrestrictive clause. A restrictive clause (begins with *that*) identifies the noun that comes before it and is essential to the meaning of the sentence. If you leave the clause out, it will change the meaning of the sentence. A restrictive clause does not require the use of commas to set it apart from the rest of the sentence. A nonrestrictive clause (begins with *which*) is one that merely adds information to the sentence; it is not essential and you can leave it out. A nonrestrictive clause requires commas to set it apart from the rest of the sentence.

> **Example:**
> *Improper:* Rehabilitation programs, which fail to reduce recidivism, will lose their funding.
> *Proper:* Rehabilitation programs that fail to reduce recidivism will lose their funding.

In the preceding example, the correct word is *that* because the following clause is restrictive. It identifies which programs will lose their funding and, therefore, is essential to the meaning of the sentence. Note that commas are not used to set the phrase apart from the rest of the sentence.

> **Example:**
> *Improper:* The prison, that was built in 1990, has both male and female inmates.
> *Proper:* The prison, which was built in 1990, has both male and female inmates.

In this example, the correct word is *which* because the clause that follows is nonrestrictive. It does not identify the noun that comes before it, and the clause is not essential to the meaning of the sentence. It adds detail, but deleting it will not change the meaning of the sentence. Note that commas are used to set the phrase apart from the rest of the sentence.

If you are having a difficult time deciding which word to use, ask yourself if the meaning of the sentence will change if you leave the clause out. If the answer is yes, it is a restrictive clause and the correct word to use is *that*, with no commas preceding or following it. If the answer is no, it is a nonrestrictive clause, and the correct word to use is *which*, with a comma preceding it and another comma at the end of the clause.

> See **Mechanics of Writing, Class Exercise #4 "Identifying Mechanical and Grammatical Errors"** at the end of this unit.

Assembling Your Final Paper: From the Title Page to the Reference List

After you have finished writing and editing your paper, and before you proofread it, you must create a title page, add a running head with page numbers, and attach the reference list.

Creating a Title Page

You must include a title page with your paper. To create a title page, follow these rules:

1. Compose a title that is a concise statement summarizing the main idea of your paper. It should be no more than 12 words and it should be formal; do not write a creative, flowery title to impress your readers. Remember—this is an academic paper.
2. Center your title and type it in the top half of the page.
3. Use the same font style and size that you use in the body of your paper; do not make it bold, enclose it in quotation marks, or underline it.

4. Capitalize the first letter of each word, except for words such as *and, of, on*, and *to*. According to the *Publication Manual* (6th edition), you must also capitalize all words that are four letters or more, such as *from* and *that*. There are many rules about capitalization; for a more detailed discussion on which words to capitalize, see the *Publication Manual* (6th edition), Section 4.15.

5. Type your name, the course name or number, and the date in the center of the lower half of the page. This information must also be presented in the same font style and size that you use in the body of your paper.

Creating a Running Head With Page Numbers

Before you proofread your paper, you must insert a running head with page numbers. The running head and the page numbers should both be placed in the upper right-hand corner of each page of your paper, starting with the title page. The running head should be composed of the first four to seven words of your title and typed in all capital letters. Different computer programs require different steps for inserting running heads with page numbers; if you have questions about how to do this, click on the HELP button of the word processing program on your computer.

> See **Mechanics of Writing, Handout #3: "Sample Title Page"** at the end of this unit.

Attaching the Reference List

The final step in assembling your paper is to attach the reference list. Typically, students create the reference list as a separate document; remember to attach it to the end of your paper and to add the proper running head and page number(s) to it.

Proofreading Your Paper: The Final Step

After you have written and edited several drafts of your paper and you feel that it is finished, you must proofread it on both a global and a local level before you hand it in. This will be the final step in preparing your paper.

When you proofread your paper, you must focus on all of the guidelines you have learned in this unit (e.g., organization, sentence structure), as enumerated in the next section. To help you remember what to look for as you proofread your paper, refer to the following handout.

> See **Mechanics of Writing, Handout #4: "Research Paper Checklist"** at the end of this unit.

Proofreading: General Rules

When you proofread your paper, follow these general rules:

1. *Proofread a hard copy.* Your eye will catch more errors if you read a hard copy than if you read it on a computer screen.
2. *Read your paper out loud.* Your ear will catch mistakes that your eyes may miss.
3. *Concentrate on only a few elements at a time.* When you read through your paper, you will need to look at a lot of elements. To ensure that you do not miss errors,

concentrate on only a few elements at a time. Although this will require you to read through your paper several times, you will catch more errors than if you try to look for everything at once.

4. *Do not fix the errors as you find them.* As you find errors, circle them but do not stop to fix them. Doing so will cause you to lose momentum. After you have read through your paper and circled all of the errors, you will go back through and correct them.

5. *Do not wait until the last minute to proofread your paper.* Proofreading your paper properly will take time. If you rush, you will miss errors.

Proofreading Your Paper: A Checklist

When you proofread your paper, follow these steps:

- ☐ 1. *Proofread the overall format of the paper.* As you read through it, consider these questions:
    - ☐ a. Do you have an introduction, a discussion, and a conclusion?
    - ☐ b. Is your spacing correct? Are your margins the proper width (the default setting of the word processing program), does your paper start at the top of page 1, did you hit ENTER only once between paragraphs, and do you have enough information to meet the paper's page requirement?
    - ☐ c. Are your paragraphs an acceptable length? Do you have at least three sentences per paragraph, and are they not overly long?
    - ☐ d. Did you number all of your pages?
- ☐ 2. *Proofread for sentence-level errors.* Proofread your paper by reading it out loud; your ear will catch mistakes that your eyes may miss. Circle errors as you find them, but do not stop to fix them. You will go back and fix them after you have finished reading your paper.

    As you read your paper, consider these questions:
    - ☐ a. If you are writing an argumentative paper, did you include your thesis statement in your first paragraph? If you are writing an analytical paper, did you include your research question in your first paragraph?
    - ☐ b. Are your punctuation and spelling correct?
    - ☐ c. Did you include only one idea in each paragraph?
    - ☐ d. Did you include topic sentences for every paragraph?
    - ☐ e. Did you use transition words in your paragraphs?
- ☐ 3. *Proofread citations.* Make sure you have properly and completely cited all sources in correct APA format, consistent with the *Publication Manual* (6th edition). Remember that you must cite everything that is not common knowledge. If you have not included a citation where you stated something that is not common knowledge, you will need to add it. In addition, compare the citations in your paper with those on your reference list to make sure they match.
- ☐ 4. *Have a third party read your paper.* After you have finished proofreading your paper, have a friend read it to see if it makes sense. (Ask someone who has good writing skills.) If something does not make sense to that person, it will probably not make sense to the instructor either, and you should revise that section. This step requires that you park your ego at the door! Do not be offended if you do not like your friend's feedback. Remember, you will make the final decision as to whether you take your friend's advice; if you do not like his or her suggestion, do not use it.

Unit 5 | Mechanics of Writing: From the First Draft to the Final Paper

☐ 5. *Save your work.* Save a copy of your paper to an external source, such as to "the cloud" or a flash drive, and print out an extra copy. This ensures that you will have a copy in case anything happens to your original.

> *See* **Mechanics of Writing, Class Exercise #5: "Editing Exercise"** *at the end of this unit.*

> *See* **Mechanics of Writing, Handout #5: "Grammar Reference Guide"** *at the end of this unit.*

> *See* **Mechanics of Writing, Take-Home Assignment #1: "Editing a Paper"** *at the end of this unit.*

NOTES

Mechanics of Writing, Class Exercise #1

Identifying Mechanical Errors

Read the following sentences. Each contains a style error. Errors may include the use of informal or emotional language, improper tone (e.g., first person), or wordiness. Rewrite each sentence so it is correct, without changing the meaning of the sentence.

1. It is evident that youths commit high numbers of crimes.

2. In the year of 2010, more men were arrested than women.

3. We, as a society, are responsible for the welfare of our kids.

4. It is imperative that we punish rapists more severely.

5. Young male juveniles have a greater number of participation in street crimes than young female juveniles.

6. Sadly, for the years between 2011 and 2013, assault was the most common type of crime committed by juveniles.

7. According to experts, forcing a child who was sexually assaulted to testify in court is totally inappropriate.

Mechanics of Writing, Class Exercise #1

8. In the year of 2013, there were approximately 123 million episodes in which individuals got behind the wheel of a car and operated the motor vehicle while under the influence of alcohol.

_____

_____

_____

_____

Mechanics of Writing, Class Exercise #2

Topic Sentences

Read the following paragraphs. Then write a topic sentence for each of them.

1. One benefit of good-time credit is that inmates' sentences are reduced, which reduces prison overcrowding. Another benefit is that inmates who receive good-time credit for attending GED classes increase their levels of education. Finally, good-time credit encourages inmates to behave, and, as a result, the number of violent acts between inmates decreases.

   _____

   _____

2. One animal rehabilitation program in prisons involves service dogs. Another program involves wild horses. A third program involves small animals, such as rabbits. Regardless of the type of animal, research has shown that animal rehabilitation programs help inmates increase their levels of self-esteem.

   _____

   _____

Mechanics of Writing, Class Exercise #3

Selecting Correct Transition Words

Fill in the correct transition word for each example.

1. Most inmates who attend GED class are eligible for good-time credit. _____ if an inmate misbehaves in class, he or she will lose that benefit.
    a. Moreover,
    b. However,
    c. In addition,
    d. In conclusion,

2. Typically, a police officer will give first-time teenage curfew violators a warning not to do it again. _____ the officer will have the youths call their parents.
    a. Therefore,
    b. On the other hand,
    c. In contrast,
    d. In addition,

3. All police canines live with the officers who trained them. _____ they form a bond that allows them to work together as a team.
    a. Finally,
    b. In other words,
    c. Likewise,
    d. As a result,

4. The man entered the house through an unlocked window. _____ he stole many valuable items.
    a. Likewise,
    b. Specifically,
    c. Subsequently,
    d. Accordingly,

5. When police officers stop people whom they suspect of driving under the influence, the officers have the drivers take a sobriety test. _____ the officers may ask the drivers to walk a straight line.
    a. In particular,
    b. However,
    c. In contrast,
    d. In addition,

Mechanics of Writing, Class Exercise #4

Identifying Mechanical and Grammatical Errors, Part I

Part I: Look at the underlined words in each sentence and determine whether they are mechanically and grammatically correct. If they are incorrect, rewrite them so they are mechanically and grammatically correct. If they are correct, write okay *by the underlined word(s).*

1. Since the <u>1990's</u>, there has been an increase in the <u>amount</u> of teenagers who leave school before tenth grade.

2. The inmates <u>didn't</u> like the movie <u>due to the fact that</u> it was about politics, which they found to be boring.

3. <u>There is no doubt about the fact that</u> crime rates are an important topic in <u>our</u> society.

4. According to the prison administrator, "<u>Twelve</u> inmates were put into solitary confinement for <u>fighting"</u>.

5. After the data <u>was</u> gathered, the researchers discovered that <u>they're</u> study was flawed.

Mechanics of Writing, Class Exercise #4

Identifying Mechanical and Grammatical Errors, Part II

Part II: Read the following sentences and determine whether they are mechanically and grammatically correct. If they are incorrect, rewrite them so they are free of mechanical and grammatical errors. If they are correct as written, write okay *by the sentence.*

1. The man was chased by the police officer.

2. At the men's detention center, after each inmate ate breakfast, they went to work.

3. It was found by researchers that three percent of all boys become truant from school.

4. Because several inmates were sick, the GED teacher cancelled their class.

5. The teens that were involved in the altercation were arrested.

6. The cop approached the man, drew his gun, and was ordering him to put up his hands.

7. Tragically, the boy who was assaulted by the man who is married to his mother, was seriously hurt.

Mechanics of Writing, Class Exercise #5

Editing Exercise

Edit the following three paragraphs. You do not need to rewrite the sentences, but you do need to correct all mechanical and grammatical errors that you find. Further, if citations are missing, note where they should be included.

In 1816, Georgia law allowed for an african american to be put to death for the rape of a white woman. If a white man committed the same crime against an African American woman, his punishment was too pay a fine (Smith, 2010). Since the 1930's ninety percent of those people sentenced to death for crimes such as rape have been African American (White, 2012).

Executions were brought to a halt in the US in 1972 when the Supreme Court held that the death penalty was being given disproportionately to defendants that were African American and that most white defendants were let off the hook. Giving researchers time to research the death penalty (Jones, 2012). Ultimately, the death penalty was reinstated many years later.

In conclusion, historically the death penalty was disproportionately applied against African Americans. Poorer people were also sentenced to die more frequently than those with money (Marks, 2014). Although society has tried to fix this problem, studies show that most people executed in our county are African American. This is not acceptable!

Mechanics of Writing, Handout #1

Transition Words and Phrases

To conclude (Because of this . . . then this):

Therefore	Consequently	It follows that
As a result	Accordingly	For this reason
Hence	Thus	

Example: Drunk driving is a serious issue. _____, harsher drunk-driving laws must be passed.

To illustrate or explain an idea:

For example	In particular	Specifically
To illustrate	For instance	

Example: There are many types of "street drugs." _____, one is marijuana.

To add a new point:

Moreover	Further	Also
In addition	And	Furthermore

Example: All of the inmates are men. _____, they are all under the age of 21.

To list items of information or items relating to time:

Subsequently   Next
First (second, third)   Then
Last (requires at least two previous items in the list)
Finally (requires at least two previous items in the list)

Example: In the morning, juvenile boot camp participants first eat breakfast. _____, they clean their living areas, _____ they go to school.

To repeat or restate a similar idea:

To repeat   In other words

Example: Ten percent of the offenders were female. _____, one-tenth of the offenders were female.

To indicate a conclusion:

In conclusion   In sum   In summary

Example: _____, more prisons must be built in order to alleviate the overcrowding problem.

To indicate a similarity:

Similarly   Likewise

Example: The leading cause of death for children is automobile accidents. _____, many young adults are also killed in car accidents.

To indicate a difference:

In contrast   However
On the contrary   But
On the one hand/On the other hand

Example: Many offenders recidivate. _____, many do not.

Mechanics of Writing, Handout #2

Sample Paragraphs

Sample introduction (Thesis statement: *To reduce overcrowding and taxpayer liability, private entities should take over the prison industry.*):

Over the past 15 years, the United States has witnessed a dramatic increase in its prison population. In particular, the number of inmates has increased from 200,000 to 1.5 million. As a result, prisons suffer from overcrowding and taxpayers must pay billions of dollars annually to house these inmates. To reduce overcrowding and taxpayer liability, private entities should take over the prison industry.

Sample topic sentence (Statistics are from the U.S. Census Bureau, Population Division, 2014):

Criminal justice researchers must address the issue of elder abuse because the elderly population has increased dramatically over the past several decades. In particular, in 2012, approximately 13% of the population was over the age of 65. Researchers project that by 2050, the number of elderly in this country will double. With this increase in population, it is likely that the number of incidents of elder abuse will also increase. As a result, researchers must examine the issue of elder abuse so that interventions can be created to address it.

Sample conclusion:

Over the past few years, prisons have introduced the use of animals into their rehabilitation programs. Because these programs are still new, few studies have been conducted that examine their effectiveness at reducing recidivism rates. However, preliminary research suggests that these programs are highly effective. Accordingly, prisons with high recidivism rates should consider implementing one of these programs at their institutions.

Mechanics of Writing, Handout #3

Sample Title Page

A sample of a proper title page appears on the following page. There are several things you should note about the sample title page:

- The running head and the page number are located at the top, right-hand corner of the page. The running head is typed in capital letters.
- The title is short and centered on the top half of the page; only the major words are capitalized.
- The author's name, course name and number, and date are centered in the bottom half of the page.

EXPOSURE TO COMMUNITY VIOLENCE 1

Exposure to Community Violence and Its Effect on Juvenile Delinquency Patterns

Jane Doe
CRJU 304
November 22, 2015

Mechanics of Writing, Handout #4

Research Paper Checklist

Before you hand in your paper, go through this checklist to make sure your paper includes all of the required elements and that it complies with this list.

- ☐ 1. *Ideas and content.* Your paper presents a thorough review of the literature and discusses all of the criteria specified by your instructor. (Typically, this includes a description or definition of the program or policy, the scope of the problem it was designed to address, the history, the targeted population, its purpose or goals, and its activities or elements).
- ☐ 2. *Discussion of the studies.* Each study includes the name of the program or policy examined and discusses all of the criteria specified by your instructor. (Typically, this includes the purpose of the study or research question, the targeted population, the methods by which the researchers got their data, the researchers' findings, and the stated limitations, if any).
- ☐ 3. *Document organization.* Your paper has an introduction and conclusion of appropriate lengths with appropriate content, presents the material in a logical order, and does not violate the "clumping rule."
- ☐ 4. *Paragraph coherence.* There is one idea or topic per paragraph, transitions are used between paragraphs, sentences are presented in a logical sequence, and paragraphs are of an appropriate length.
- ☐ 5. *Sentence structure.* You express ideas clearly, use topic sentences and transition words, and do not use awkward or run-on sentences.
- ☐ 6. *Mechanics and proofreading.* You use proper grammar and mechanics and also use correct spelling, punctuation, and spacing.
- ☐ 7. *Paraphrase of material.* Your content is well paraphrased, and your paper has no direct quotes or material that is too similar to the original.
- ☐ 8. *Citations.* Your paper includes citations where necessary, citations in the text match citations on the reference list, and citations are written in proper APA format in the text and on the reference list.

Mechanics of Writing, Handout #5

Grammar Reference Guide

Sentence Structure

1. Write simple, concise sentences.
2. Avoid redundancy.
3. Avoid stilted sentences; vary your language.
4. Do not use flowery or grandiose language or exaggerate facts.
5. Do not use contractions.
6. Do not use informal language or slang.
7. Do not write in the first person (e.g., "I," "we," "our," "us").
8. Check that each noun (singular or plural) matches its pronoun.
9. Use the active voice instead of passive voice.
10. When presenting other people's research, write the findings in the past tense.
11. Check for parallel sentence structure (e.g., "between...and"; "neither...nor"; "either...or").
12. Use the same verb tenses in a sentence (parallelism; e.g., The judge banged his gavel, ordered the defendant to sit down, and instructed the jury to disregard the outburst.).
13. Place periods and commas inside quotation marks.
14. Watch the length of your paragraphs—a minimum of three sentences, and no more than three-quarters of a page.

Errors to Avoid

1. Watch for *its* versus *it's*. *It's* = *it is* or *it has*.
2. Plural dates (e.g., 1980s) do not have an apostrophe.
3. The word *data* is plural.
4. Know the difference between commonly confused words: *between* versus *among*; *since* versus *because*; *number* versus *amount*; *who* versus *that*; *then* versus *than*; *there* versus *their* versus *they're*.
5. Do not write out *percent* when it is preceded by a numeral; use %.
6. Do not use slashes (e.g., *he/she*, *and/or*).
7. Use *he* or *she* for a singular pronoun, not *their*.
8. Write out all numbers less than 10 (general rule). Review *Publication Manual* (6th edition), Sections 4.33–4.34, for exceptions.

Mechanics of Writing, Take-Home Assignment #1

Editing a Paper

Using the rules you have learned so far in this unit, edit a paper you have written and handed in for a previous class. It must be a paper in which you were required to include citations. You must edit the paper on *both* a global and a local level. Make comments in the margins about problems you see with it, including organization, grammar, mechanics, and missing citations. *The more detailed your comments, the better your grade will be!* In addition, score yourself on each item in the following grading rubric, using the criteria listed on the rubric and the information that you have learned in this unit. Staple the completed rubric to the front of your paper.

Student Grading Rubric for Mechanics of Writing, Take-Home Assignment #1				
CRITERIA	EXCELLENT 4	GOOD 3	ACCEPTABLE 2	NEEDS IMPROVEMENT 1
Global Editing:				
Ideas and Content				
Organization				
Local Editing:				
Organization				
Sentence Fluency				
Proofreading				
Citation				

Global Editing

1. *Ideas and Content*: Is there a sufficient amount of discussion about the topic? Is it clear that the writer read and understood the research?
2. *Organization*: Did the writer organize his or her paper well on a global level? Did the writer include a thesis statement in the first paragraph? Was the content organized into logical sections? Was the paper formatted correctly (e.g., numbered pages; correct margin sizes)?

Local Editing

1. *Organization*: Did the writer use topic sentences? Did the writer include only one idea per paragraph? Did the writer comply with the "clumping rule"? Did the writer use transitional words to link sentences and transitional sentences to link connecting paragraphs?
2. *Sentence Fluency*: Did the writer follow the mechanics and grammar rules discussed in class? Did the writer write clearly and concisely? Are there awkward sentences?
3. *Proofreading*: Did the writer make spelling, spacing, or grammatical errors? Are there any other errors that he or she should have caught before turning in the paper?
4. *Citations*: Did the writer use complete and correct citations? Did the writer include citations everywhere they were required?

Writing an Annotation

UNIT 6

UNIT SUMMARY
Learning Objectives
Writing an Annotation: An Overview
Rules for Writing an Annotation
Two Types of Commonly Annotated Criminal Justice Sources
    Empirical Studies
    Research Reports
Approach to Writing an Annotation

Learning Objectives

At the end of this unit, students will be able to do the following:
- Write an annotation.
- Correctly interpret an empirical study.

Writing an Annotation: An Overview

There are several important introductory facts about annotations:

1. An annotation is a short summary that explains, describes, or evaluates a source.
2. An annotation can vary in length from one paragraph to several pages.
3. The purpose of an annotation is to inform the reader of the relevance, accuracy, and quality of the source cited.
4. There are two types of annotations:
   a. A descriptive annotation. This type of annotation merely describes the content of the work without critiquing or judging it. It is the type of annotation you will learn how to write in this unit.
   b. A critical annotation. This type of annotation both describes and evaluates the source. For example, the annotation might note how the research has or has not contributed to the field. Similarly, it may point out the biases of the author(s) or the limitations of the methodology or findings.

Typically, as a criminal justice student, you will not write just a single annotation. Instead, you will create an annotated bibliography, which is a bibliography with annotations for each source. There are two types of annotated bibliographies:

1. The first type simply summarizes the research that has been published on a specific topic, so students can gain a perspective on what researchers have previously found.
2. The second type is an *evaluative* annotated bibliography, which presents a critical summary of the current research. When you create this type of bibliography, you evaluate each source on its own merits and compare it to, and critique it against, the other research included in your annotated bibliography.

There are several reasons for writing an annotated bibliography:

1. It can provide you with the opportunity to learn more about a topic.
2. It can help you begin to frame a thesis statement. Students often have a general idea of the topic they would like to write about in their papers but struggle with the specific direction they would like to take. By reading a cross-section of the relevant research, you can explore the different issues that have been identified in the literature. This will help you begin to frame your thesis statement and decide which direction your paper should take.

Note! Do not confuse an annotation with an abstract. Although the two may seem similar, they are actually very different. Specifically, an annotation typically includes a description or summary of the contents of a publication. It may also include an evaluation of that content. In contrast, an abstract provides only an objective description of the contents of a publication.

Rules for Writing an Annotation

When you write an annotation, you should follow these six rules:

1. Use full sentences that are grammatically correct when writing an annotation. In other words, you must follow the mechanical rules that you previously learned (e.g., write a minimum of three sentences per paragraph, use transition words, and write concisely without slang).
2. You must write your annotation in an essay format; however, you do not have to have an introduction or a conclusion. You need introductions and conclusions only when you write academic papers and formal essays.
3. You must completely paraphrase all of the information you include in the annotation. Failure to completely paraphrase the material is plagiarism.
4. As you paraphrase the material, be careful not to change the meaning of the information.

> **Note!** Do not change the names of the variables by using synonyms; if you do, you will change their meaning.

5. Write your annotation based on the information contained in the article. Do not rely on the information in the abstract alone.
6. Double-space the annotation, using default margins.

Two Types of Commonly Annotated Criminal Justice Sources

As a criminal justice student, the two types of sources you will most likely annotate are empirical studies and research reports.

Empirical Studies

"Empirical studies are reports of original research" (APA *Publication Manual*, 6th edition, 2010, p. 10). In empirical studies, researchers analyze either primary or secondary data, report their findings, draw conclusions, and make suggestions for future research. Empirical studies are typically published in scholarly journals.

Empirical studies have specific sections, and a good way to determine if your source is an empirical study is to look for these sections: the introduction, method, results (sometimes called "analysis" or "findings"), discussion, and conclusion. Each section may include some or all of the following information:

1. Introduction: The introduction gives a brief history of the problem being examined, a literature review of relevant studies, and the purpose of the current study.
2. Method: This section discusses who participated in the study, how the researchers obtained their data, the definitions of the variables, and the types of analyses used.
3. Results: This section discusses the statistical findings and analyses in formal, often quantitative, language.
4. Discussion: This section discusses all of the findings previously discussed in the results section, but in simpler language.
5. Conclusion: This section is a summary of the findings, and it proposes directions for future research.

Empirical studies typically examine and analyze several variables. When you read an empirical study, you should focus only on the variables that are relevant to your thesis statement or to the topic of your paper.

> **Example:**
>
> You are writing a paper about the success of treatment programs for drunk drivers. The study examines the recidivism rates of drunk-driving offenders who completed treatment programs and the recidivism rates of those who received punishment. When you read the empirical study, you should focus only on the discussion and findings concerning treatment; do not focus on the discussion about punishment.

Research Reports

A research report is typically published by a government agency such as the Bureau of Justice Statistics, U.S. Department of Justice, or National Institute of Justice. Like empirical studies, research reports are grounded in research and can include either primary or secondary data. However, research reports do not always follow the format previously described for empirical studies.

Research reports include a literature review or background discussion of the subject and a description of where the data came from and how they were gathered. However, they might not include a separate discussion of the analytical techniques used to evaluate the data. Further, they often present simply a summary of the findings rather than a detailed discussion about them.

 Some research reports present the results of an outcome or evaluation study, and other research reports focus just on how a program or policy was implemented. When you conduct your library research for an academic paper, the empirical studies you find may be presented in research reports or journal articles.

Approach to Writing an Annotation

To write an effective annotation for the handouts at the end of this unit, follow these steps:

1. Read the entire source document; do not rely only on the abstract. Also, do not simply search through the article for the answers to the questions. If you do that, you will be taking points out of context, which might cause you to draw incorrect conclusions.

2. On a separate piece of paper, or in a blank Word document, answer the annotation questions contained in the handouts at the end of this unit, or those provided to you by your instructor. These questions direct you to the important parts of the article. When you receive an assignment to write an annotation for another class, you can use these questions as a guide to help you find the important information in those articles.

3. Using your answers to the questions, write the first draft of your annotation. Remember, you must follow the mechanical and grammatical rules previously discussed (e.g., essay format, topic sentences, no contractions, transition words).

4. Do not include information from the source that you do not understand. If you do not understand something, your paraphrase will most likely not make sense.

5. Always include the question in your answer.

Approach to Writing an Annotation

Example:
The first question asks you to identify the researchers. Your answer should state, "*In this article, the researchers are Oakley and Wilson.*"

Warning! When you answer the questions, you must completely paraphrase the information. Do not copy the answers directly from the source because that is plagiarism. If you do not have time to paraphrase the information at this point, put quotation marks around the directly quoted information and make a large note to yourself that it is a direct quote. You must go back and rewrite the information in your own words, later.

6. When you write the first draft of the annotation, focus simply on getting all of the answers down on paper (or in your Word document). Do not revise and rewrite as you go; after you have written the first draft, you will have an opportunity to make revisions when you edit it.
7. After you have written the first draft, go back through and edit it, following the steps for editing that you have previously learned.
8. Your final draft must be double-spaced, with default margins, and in essay format.

Note! When you write an annotation, or an annotated bibliography, the length of the annotation may vary from one paragraph to several pages, depending on the type of annotation you are asked to write (e.g., a descriptive annotation or a critical annotation).

*See **Writing an Annotation, Class Exercise #1: "Annotation Questions for Alcohol-Impaired Driving Article"** and **Writing an Annotation: "General Questions for Writing an Annotation"** at the end of this unit.*

*If your instructor assigns you the annotation writing assignment for the Domestic Violence Abusers article as a take-home assignment, see **Writing an Annotation, Take-Home Assignment #1: "Annotation Questions for Domestic Violence Abusers Article"** at the end of this unit. If your instructor assigns you a different article as a take-home assignment, see **Writing an Annotation: "General Questions for Writing an Annotation"** at the end of this unit.*

Note! *If an instructor in another class assigns you to write an annotation, use **"Writing an Annotation: General Questions for Writing an Annotation"** at the end of this unit as a guide.*

NOTES

Writing an Annotation, Class Exercise #1

Annotation Questions for Alcohol-Impaired Driving Article

Read the article cited below and then write your answers to the following questions. In class, we will use the answers as a guideline to write a one-page annotation. When you answer the questions, all of the information must come from the text, not from the abstract. Also, you must paraphrase the information in your answers; do not directly copy it from the article.

Liu, S., Siegel, P. Z., Brewer, R. D., Mokdad, A. H., Sleet, D. A., & Serdula, M. (1997). Prevalence of alcohol-impaired driving: Results from a national self-reported survey of health behaviors. *Journal of the American Medical Association, 277*(2), 122–125.

1. What type of source is this?

   _____

2. Who were the researchers and what was the purpose of their study?

   _____
   _____
   _____

3. How did the researchers obtain their data? Briefly state where the data came from.

   _____
   _____
   _____

4. What did the researchers find? In other words,
   a. What did they find with regard to the number of participants who drove while impaired by alcohol?

   _____
   _____

   b. What generalizations did they make, based on that number?

   _____
   _____

   c. Which participants did they find were the most likely to drink and drive?

   _____

5. What did the researchers conclude from their findings?

   _____
   _____
   _____

Writing an Annotation, Class Exercise #1

6. What were the limitations of the study? Specifically, what factors may have influenced the researchers' findings?

   _____
   _____
   _____

7. What recommendations did the researchers make to help reduce the number of incidents of drunk driving?

   _____
   _____
   _____

Writing an Annotation

General Questions for Writing an Annotation

Read the assigned article and then write your answers to the following questions. You will use the answers as a guideline to write an annotation. When you answer the questions, all of the information must come from the text, not *from the abstract. Also, you must paraphrase the information in your answers; do not directly copy it from the article.*

1. What type of source is this?

2. Who were the researchers?

3. What was the purpose of the study (what were the research questions)?

4. How did the researchers obtain their data?

5. What did the researchers find?

6. What did the researchers conclude from their findings?

7. What were the limitations of the study? Specifically, what factors may have influenced the researchers' findings?

Writing an Annotation

8. What did the researchers suggest for future research?

_____

_____

_____

Writing an Annotation, Take-Home Assignment #1

Annotation Questions for Domestic Violence Abusers Article

Read the article cited below, then answer the following questions. Use those answers as a guideline to write your annotation. Be sure to write your annotation in complete sentences with proper grammar and to paraphrase completely the information in your own words. Failing to paraphrase completely or copying any information directly from the original article constitutes plagiarism. Further, all information you use must come from the text, not *from the abstract.*

Etter, G. W., Sr., & Birzer, M. L. (2007). Domestic violence abusers: A descriptive study of the characteristics of defenders in protection from abuse orders in Sedgwick County, Kansas. *Journal of Family Violence, 22*, 113–119. doi: 10.1007/s10896-006-9047-x

1. What type of source is this?

2. Who were the researchers?

3. How did the researchers obtain their data? Briefly state where the data came from.

4. What three research questions did the researchers examine?

5. What did the researchers find? You must state at least one finding that directly relates to each research question.

6. What were the limitations of the study? Specifically, what factors may have influenced the researchers' findings? You must state at least three limitations.

Writing an Annotation, Take-Home Assignment #1

7. What did the researchers suggest for future research? You must state at least three suggestions.

Creating a Reference List in APA Style

UNIT 7

UNIT SUMMARY
Learning Objectives
APA-Style Reference List: An Overview
Citations on the Reference List
    General Formatting Rules
    Citing Authors
        Citations With One Author
        Citations With Two Authors
        Citations With Three to Seven Authors
        Citations With Eight or More Authors
        Special Circumstances When Citing Two or More Authors
    Citing the Date of Publication
        Citing a Single Author With Works Published in Different Years
        Citing a Single Author With Several Works Published in the Same Year
    Citing the Title of a Journal Article
    Citing the Title of a Journal
    Citing the Volume and Issue Numbers
    Citing the Pages of a Journal Article
    The Finished Citation
Citations for Different Types of Sources
    Print Sources
        Journal Article
        Research Report
        Book
        Article or Chapter in an Edited Book
    Electronic Sources
        Article From a Website
        Article From a Database With a DOI Number
        Article From a Database Without a DOI Number

Learning Objectives

At the end of this unit, students will be able to do the following:

- Identify the difference between a bibliography and a reference list.
- Prepare a reference list in APA style, in accordance with the *Publication Manual* (6th edition).

APA-Style Reference List: An Overview

There are several important introductory facts about reference lists:

- The purpose of a reference list is to give readers information about the sources so they can locate copies of those they wish to read.
- A reference list is not the same as a bibliography. A reference list includes only the sources you actually used, and cited, in your paper. A bibliography includes all of the sources you reviewed for your paper, regardless of whether you actually used them.
- Every source you cite in the text of your paper must be listed on your reference list. Similarly, every source you list on your reference list must be cited in your paper.

There are many *Publication Manual* rules about citations on the reference list. You will learn how to cite the most commonly used sources. For all other citation types, or for questions you may have about citing, refer to the *Publication Manual* (6th edition). You can also go to www.apastyle.org/learn/index.aspx for further information about citing sources in APA style.

Citations on the Reference List

General Formatting Rules

1. Center the title at the top of the page in the same size and style font as used in the rest of your paper.
2. The correct title is References, not Reference List, Bibliography, Reference, or Works Cited. (Works Cited is used only for an MLA-style reference list.)
3. Capitalize only the first letter of References. Do not bold, italicize, or underline the title.
4. Do not number the entries on the reference list.
5. Double-space the reference list entries. Do not add an extra line space between each source entry.
6. Begin each entry with a hanging indent. To do this, begin each source flush with the left-hand margin. When you are finished typing all of the information for the citation, format the entry so the second line of text and all subsequent lines for that entry are indented. (This is most easily done by formatting the entire list after all the entries have been typed.)

Example:

Lee, J. M., Steinberg, L., & Piquero, A. R. (2010). Ethnic identity and attitudes toward the police among African American juvenile offenders. *Journal of Criminal Justice, 38*(4), 781–789.

Citations on the Reference List

7. Insert a single space between each of the elements in a citation (e.g., between the last author's initial and the date).
8. Present the sources alphabetically by the first author's last name.
9. Do not change the order of the authors within a citation on the reference list. Include them on the reference list in the same order in which they are listed in the original source.
10. In general, most sources you will cite will contain the same elements. These are the author(s), year of publication, title, and publisher information or data required to retrieve the source.

In the next section of this unit, we will discuss the particular rules for each of these elements, using a journal article citation as an example.

Citing Authors

The first element of a citation on the reference list is the name(s) of the author(s). When you write a citation, always use the name(s) of the author(s) on the original source and not from the abstract in the database; the abstract does not always list all of the authors, especially when there are more than three. If you rely on the abstract for the name(s) of the author(s), your reference list might be incorrect.

Citations With One Author

Write the last name followed by the first initial of the author's first name and a middle initial if one is given; do *not* include first or middle names. In addition, if there is a middle initial, include a space between the initials. If the author's name includes "Jr." or a number (e.g., III), you must include it. However, do not include credentials such as JD or MD.

> **Examples of citations with one author:**
>
> One author—Wilson, K. W.
>
> Note that you use only initials; do not write first or middle names. In addition, note that there is a space between the "K." and the "W."
>
> One author with "Jr."—Wilson, K. W., Jr.
>
> Note that there is a comma after the middle initial and before the "Jr."

Citations With Two Authors

If there are two authors, list both and separate the names with an ampersand (&). Include a comma before the ampersand.

> **Example of a citation with two authors:**
>
> Wilson, L. M., & Oakley, S. K.

Citations With Three to Seven Authors

If there are three to seven authors, you must list all of the authors and put an ampersand before the name of the last author. Include a comma before the ampersand.

> **Example of a citation with three to seven authors:**
>
> Oakley, T., Jackson, R., Marvin, L. S., & Summers, L. M.
>
> Note that there is a comma after the "S." and before the ampersand.

Citations With Eight or More Authors

If the citation has eight or more authors, list the first six authors followed by three ellipsis points and then the last author's last name. Include a comma before the ellipses. There is no ampersand before the last name.

> **Example of a citation with eight or more authors:**
>
> Taylor, R., Thomas, T., Jackson, L., Oakley, T., Wilson, W., Harvey, K. L., . . . Roger, Y.
>
> Note that there is a comma after the "L." and before the ellipses. There is no ampersand before the last name.

Special Circumstances When Citing Two or More Authors

Authors often publish articles with different coauthors. To cite such sources, alphabetize by the second author's last name:

> **Example:**
>
> First entry—Wilson, Y. D., & Bryce, E. B.
>
> Second entry—Wilson, Y. D., & Wells, L. F.
>
> If the second author is the same, alphabetize by the third author's last name, and so on.

Citing the Date of Publication

The next element after the name(s) of the author(s) is the date of publication. For this element, write the year of publication in parentheses. Do not include a month or season, even if one is given.

Citing a Single Author With Works Published in Different Years

Often, an author will have published several articles. If you want to cite more than one of his or her articles, cite the oldest work first.

> **Example:**
>
> J. P. Wilson published an article in 2014 and another in 2016. The entries in the references would be listed as follows:
>
> Wilson, J. P. (2014).
>
> Wilson, J. P. (2016).

Citations on the Reference List

Citing a Single Author With Several Works Published in the Same Year

Occasionally, an author may have several articles published in the same year. If this occurs and you want to use more than one article, you must look to the title of the article to determine the order of the sources on the reference list.

> **Example:**
>
> In 2015, Wilson published an article titled "An Analysis of Truancy Recidivism Data." That same year, he published an article titled "An Evaluation of a School Truancy Program." Because the word *analysis* begins with an "a," and the word *evaluation* begins with an "e," the article titled, "An Analysis of Truancy Recidivism Data" will be listed first on the reference list.
>
> When you list such sources on your reference list, you must use lowercase letters next to the publication year to differentiate them.
>
> The entries would be listed on the reference list as follows:
>
> Wilson, T. (2015a). An analysis of truancy recidivism data.
>
> Wilson, T. (2015b). An evaluation of a school truancy program.

Citing the Title of a Journal Article

In a citation to a journal article, the next element after the date of publication is the article title. The title is typed in regular font (no italics). The only capitalized words in the title are the first word, any proper nouns, and the first word of a subtitle.

> **Example:**
>
> *Article title with no subtitle:* Understanding plagiarism among college students.
>
> *Article title with a subtitle:* Understanding plagiarism among college students: Reasons why students plagiarize.

Note! Often an article title will be capitalized in the original source. Even if this is the case, follow the *Publication Manual* (6th edition) rules regarding the proper way to cite the title. Do not follow the format of the original source.

Citing the Title of a Journal

In a citation of a journal article, the next element after the article title is the journal title. The journal name is typed in italics. Each word is capitalized except for words such as *of*, *the*, *on*, and *in* (unless they are the first word of a subtitle).

> **Example:**
>
> *Journal of Criminal Justice*

Citing the Volume and Issue Numbers

In a citation of a journal article, the next element after the journal title is the volume number of the journal. The volume number is also typed in italics.

> **Example:**
>
> *Journal of Criminal Justice, 42*
>
> Note that there is a comma after the title and a space before the volume number.

After the journal volume number, cite the issue number if one is given. Not all sources will have an issue number, but if one is given, you must include it. The issue number is typed in regular font (no italics) and enclosed in parentheses. There is no space between the volume number and the issue number.

> **Example:**
>
> *Journal of Criminal Justice, 42*(2)

Citing the Pages of a Journal Article

The final element of a citation to a journal article is the page numbers of the article. You must include both the first and last page numbers. Do not write the word *pages* or the abbreviation *pp*. Instead, type only the numbers, separated by an en dash rather than a hyphen. (The en dash can be found by clicking on the symbols tab of your word processing program.) Often the abstract included in the database where you found your source will not include the last page number, so you must obtain the first and last pages from the original source. If you list only the first page, your citation will be incomplete.

> **Example:**
>
> *Journal of Criminal Justice, 42*(2), 223–242.

The Finished Citation

Using the elements discussed previously, the final citation is as follows:

> **Example:**
>
> Wilson, K. W. (2013). Understanding plagiarism among college students. *Journal of Criminal Justice, 42*(2), 223–242.

Citations for Different Types of Sources

> See **Creating a Reference List in APA Style, Handout #1: "Different Types of Sources"** at the end of this unit.

First, note the format of the citations. In particular, the citations must be typed with a hanging indent.

Print Sources
Journal Article

Lee, J. M., Steinberg, L., & Piquero, A. R. (2010). Ethnic identity and attitudes toward the police among African American juvenile offenders. *Journal of Criminal Justice, 38*(4), 781–789.

Important Points

1. The first element is the names of the authors. Note that there is a comma before the ampersand. Note also that there is only one ampersand and it is before the last author. Do not include first or middle names; include only the initials. If the author includes his or her middle initial, you must include it. Also, if the author has "Jr." or a number (e.g., III) in his or her name, you must include that. Remember to refer to the original source for the authors' names, because the abstract in the database where you found your source will not always list all of the authors.
2. The next element is the publication date. Note that the year is in parentheses.
3. The next element is the title of the article. Note that the only capitalized words are the first word and "African American," which is a proper noun. If there were a subtitle, it would be included and you would capitalize the first word of the subtitle.
4. The next element is the title of the journal. Note that the title is italicized and each word is capitalized except for the "of."
5. The next element is the volume number (here, it is 38). Note that the volume is italicized. Do not write "vol." or "volume." Simply write the number.
6. The next element is the issue number (here, it is 4). Note that it is not italicized, it is within parentheses, and there is no space between it and the volume number. Not all sources will have an issue number; however, you must include it if one is given.
7. The last element is the page numbers. You must include the first and last page numbers. Note that there is a comma after the issue number (or volume number if there is no issue number) and before the page numbers. Do not write "pages" or "pp." Simply write the page numbers. (Remember to refer to the original source for the page numbers rather than relying on the abstract from the database where you found your source.)

Research Report

Jackson, S. L., & Hafemeister, T. L. (2013). *Understanding elder abuse: New directions for developing theories of elder abuse occurring in domestic settings* (Research in Brief). Washington, DC: National Institute of Justice.

Important Points

1. As with the journal article, the first element is the names of the authors. The same rules apply to citing these authors. Note that there is a comma before the ampersand. Include only first and middle initials; do not include full names.
2. As with the journal article, the next element is the date of publication. The same rules apply to citing the date as those that apply in a journal article.
3. The next element is the title of the report. Note that the title is italicized and the only word that is capitalized is the first word of the title and the first word of the subtitle. If there were any proper nouns, you would capitalize them.
4. The next element is the Report number or Report series name. Examples of series names include "Research in Brief" and "Juvenile Justice Series." Not all reports will have a Report number or a series name; however, if a report does have a number or a series name, you must include it. Type the Report number or Publication series name in regular font, capitalize the words as you would for a title, and enclose it in parentheses. Do not put a period after the title of the report and before the Publication series name or Report number.
5. The next element is the publishing location and publisher's name. The city is listed first, followed by the two-letter postal abbreviation for the state. If you do not know what the correct abbreviation is, search for a list on the Internet. Note that there are no periods between the District of Columbia's initials; similarly, there are no periods between a state's initials. Capitalize both letters of the state's abbreviation. After the state, put a colon, then the name of the publisher.

Book

Wallace, H., & Roberson, C. (2015). *Victimology: Legal, psychological, and social perspectives* (4th ed.). Boston: Pearson.

Important Points

1. As with all of the sources discussed thus far, the first element is the names of the authors. The same rules apply as those previously discussed.
2. The next element is the date of publication. The same rules apply as those previously discussed.
3. The next element is the title of the book. Note that it is italicized, and the only capitalized words are the first word of the title and the first word of the subtitle. If the title of the book were to contain any proper nouns, you would capitalize them.
4. The next element is the edition number. Not all books will have edition numbers but if they do, you must include it. In parentheses, write the edition number (e.g., 1st, 2nd, 3rd) followed by "ed." Note that the "e" is lowercase and the "d" is followed by a period. Also note that there is a period after the parentheses.
5. The final element is the publisher's location and the name of the publisher. These are cited in the same format as the publishing information previously discussed.

Exception! According to the *Publication Manual* (6th edition), some cities do not require a state designation. You may omit the state for the following cities: Baltimore, New York, Boston, Philadelphia, Chicago, San Francisco, and Los Angeles.

Exception! According to the *Publication Manual* (6th edition), if a publisher's name includes any of the following, you should omit it from the citation: "Inc.," "Corp.," "Co.," or "Publishing." If the name includes "Press" or "Books," you must keep it.

Citations for Different Types of Sources

Example:

Chicago: University of Chicago Press.

Article or Chapter in an Edited Book

Garland, B., & Wodahl, E. (2014). Coming to a crossroads: A critical look at the sustainability of the prisoner reentry movement. In M. S. Crow & J. O. Smykla (Eds.), *Offender reentry: Rethinking criminology* (pp. 399–422). Burlington, MA: Jones and Bartlett Learning.

Important Points

1. Note that this source is an edited book—that is, one in which an editor has compiled articles written by various authors.
2. As with the previous sources, the first element is the names of the authors. The same rules apply as those previously discussed.
3. As with the previous sources, the next element is the date of publication. The same rules apply as those previously discussed.
4. The next element is the title of the article or chapter. As with the journal article, the title is typed in a regular font and the first word is capitalized, as is the first word of the subtitle. If there were any proper nouns, they would be capitalized.
5. After the title of the article, the next element is the names of the editors following the word "In." For this element, include the editor's first initial, followed by his or her last name. If a middle initial is given, you must include that as well. In parentheses, write "Ed." if there is one editor, and write "Eds." if there are two or more editors. Note that the "E" is capitalized. Also, note that the names of the two editors are separated by an ampersand. There is no comma before the ampersand. However, when there are three or more editors, separate the editors' names with commas, and place an ampersand before the last editor's first initial.
6. The next element is the title of the book. The title is italicized, and the only words that are capitalized are the first word of the title and the first word of the subtitle. If there were any proper nouns, they would be capitalized as well.
7. The next element is the page numbers of the article or chapter. For this type of source, you must type "pp." then the first and last page numbers. Enclose that information in parentheses.
8. The final element is the publishing location and publisher's name. These are cited in the same format as those cited in a research report.

Electronic Sources

Article From a Website

Shah, S., & Estrada, R. (2009). *Bridging the language divide: Promising practices for law enforcement*. Retrieved from http://www.vera.org/sites/default/files/resources/downloads/vera_bridginglang_FINAL_tagged-v2.pdf

Note! This citation is for a document obtained from an organization's website. This type of citation is different from the citation of an article that you obtain from a library's database. Do not confuse the two.

Important Points

1. As with all of the sources discussed thus far, the first element is the names of the authors. The same rules apply to citing the authors as those previously discussed.
2. The next element is the date of publication. Note that this is the copyright date, not the date on which it was retrieved from the Internet. If the article does not have a date, put "n.d." (for no date) in the place of a date. Again, the same rules apply as those we previously discussed.
3. The next element is the title of the article. Note that it is italicized and the only capitalized words are the first word of the title and the first word of the subtitle. If the title of the article were to contain any proper nouns, they also would be capitalized.
4. The next element is the URL for the article. Note that you first write "Retrieved from" and then the URL. You should copy and paste the URL into your document to ensure that you present it accurately. The computer will space to the next line if the URL does not all fit on one line.

 If you do use an article from the Internet, before you hand in your paper, make sure the URL is still current so that your reader can locate the source.

Article From a Database With a DOI Number

Stinson, P. M., Sr., Liederbach, J., & Freiburger, T. L. (2011). Off-duty and under arrest: A study of crimes perpetuated by off-duty police. *Criminal Justice Policy Review, 23*(2), 139–163. doi:10.1177/0887403410390510

This citation is to an article obtained from a library's subscription database. If a source has a DOI (digital object identifier), you must include it. When you include the DOI number, copy and paste it from the original source to ensure that it is correct.

Important Points

1. Always use lowercase letters for "doi."
2. Put a period after the last page number, but do not put a period after the DOI number.

Article From a Database Without a DOI Number

Lee, R. (2012). Community violence exposure and adolescent substance use: Does monitoring and positive parenting moderate risk in urban communities? *Journal of Community Psychology, 40*(4), 406–421. Retrieved from http://onlinelibrary.wiley.com/journal/10.1002/(ISSN)1520-6629

This citation is to an article also obtained from a library's subscription database. However, this source does not have a DOI number. Therefore, at the end of the citation, put the URL for the homepage of the journal from which you obtained the article. If you retrieved this article from your library's database, do not use that URL. Instead, do a Google search for the journal and use the URL for the homepage of the journal.

See the following handouts at the end of this unit:

Creating a Reference List in APA Style, Handout #2: "Sample Reference List"

Creating a Reference List in APA Style, Class Exercise #1: "Identifying APA Reference List Errors"

Creating a Reference List in APA Style, Take-Home Assignment #1: "Creating a Reference List for Your Paper"

NOTES

Creating a Reference List in APA Style, Class Exercise #1

Identifying APA Reference List Errors

Read through the following citations and determine what types of sources they are (e.g., journal article, book). Then determine whether the underlined words and numbers are written in correct APA format. If they are correct, write correct *above the underlined phrase. If they are incorrect, write the corrected version on the lines below the entry. After you have finished correcting the citations, look at the order of the citations. Are they in the correct order in which they should appear on a reference list? If not, write the last name of the first author in each entry in the correct order on the six numbered lines at the end of the handout.*

<u>Reference</u>

Griffin, O. H. (2014). <u>The role of the United States Supreme Court in shaping federal drug policy.</u> American Journal of Criminal Justice, <u>39(3), 660.</u>

_____

_____

<u>Dudley, R.G. (2015).</u> Childhood Trauma and its Effects: Implications For Police New Perspectives in Policing Bulletin. Washington, D.C.: U.S. Department of Justice, National Institute of Justice.

_____

_____

Kennedy, D. M. (2011). <u>Don't shoot: One man, a street fellowship, and the end of violence in inner-city America.</u> New York: Bloomsbury.

_____

_____

Sered, D. (2014, December). <u>Young men of color and the other side of harm: Addressing disparities in our responses to violence</u>. Retrieved on <u>September 24, 2015</u> from www.vera.org/pubs/men-of-color-as-victims-of-violence.

_____

_____

Creating a Reference List in APA Style, Class Exercise #1

Lee, C., & Teske, R. C. H. (2015). Specific deterrence, community context, and drunk driving: An event history analysis. *International Journal of Offender Therapy & Comparative Criminology, 59*(3), 230-258. DOI: 10.1177/0306624X14554256

_____

_____

_____

Robinson, A.L. (2015). Pie in the sky? The use of criminal justice policies and practices for intimate partner violence. In H. Johnson, B. S. Fisher, & V. Jacquier (eds.). *Critical issues on violence against women: International perspectives and promising practices.* (pages 66–76). New York: Routledge/Taylor & Francis Group.

_____

_____

_____

1. _____
2. _____
3. _____
4. _____
5. _____
6. _____

Creating a Reference List in APA Style, Handout #1

Different Types of Sources

Print Sources

Journal Article

Lee, J. M., Steinberg, L., & Piquero, A. R. (2010). Ethnic identity and attitudes toward the police among African American juvenile offenders. *Journal of Criminal Justice, 38*(4), 781–789.

Research Report

Jackson, S. L., & Hafemeister, T. L. (2013). *Understanding elder abuse: New directions for developing theories of elder abuse occurring in domestic settings* (Research in Brief). Washington, DC: National Institute of Justice.

Book

Wallace, H., & Roberson, C. (2015). *Victimology: Legal, psychological, and social perspectives* (4th ed.). Boston: Pearson.

Article or Chapter in an Edited Book

Garland, B., & Wodahl, E. (2014). Coming to a crossroads: A critical look at the sustainability of the prisoner reentry movement. In M. S. Crow & J. O. Smykla (Eds.), *Offender reentry: Rethinking criminology* (pp. 399–422). Burlington, MA: Jones and Bartlett Learning.

Electronic Sources

Article From a Website

Shah, S., & Estrada, R. (2009). *Bridging the language divide: Promising practices for law enforcement.* Retrieved from www.vera.org/sites/default/files/resources/downloads/vera_bridginglang_FINAL_tagged-v2.pdf

Article From a Database With a DOI Number

Stinson, P. M., Sr., Liederbach, J., & Freiburger, T. L. (2011). Off-duty and under arrest: A study of crimes perpetuated by off-duty police. *Criminal Justice Policy Review, 23*(2), 139–163. doi:10.1177/0887403410390510

Article From a Database Without a DOI Number

Lee, R. (2012). Community violence exposure and adolescent substance use: Does monitoring and positive parenting moderate risk in urban communities? *Journal of Community Psychology, 40*(4), 406–421.

Creating a Reference List in APA Style, Handout #2

Sample Reference List

References

Centers for Disease Control. (2015, November 24). *Impaired driving: Get the facts*. Retrieved from www.cdc.gov/motorvehiclesafety/impaired_driving/impaired- drv_factsheet.html

DeMichele, M., Lowe, N., & Payne, B. (2014). A criminological approach to explain chronic drunk driving. *American Journal of Criminal Justice, 39*(2), 292–314.

Fynbo, L. (2014). Immoral, deviant, or just normal: Drunk drivers' narratives of drinking and drunk driving. *Contemporary Drug Problems, 41*(2), 233–260.

Kamerdze, A. S., Loughran, T., Paternoster, R., & Sohoni, T. (2014). The role of affect in intended rule breaking: Extending the Rational Choice perspective. *Journal of Research in Crime and Delinquency, 51*(5), 620–654.

Lerner, B. H. (2012). *One for the road: Drunk driving since 1900*. Baltimore: Johns Hopkins University Press.

Levenson, J. S., Shields, R. T., & Singleton, D. A. (2014). Collateral punishments and sentencing policy: Perceptions of residence restrictions for sex offenders and drunk drivers. *Criminal Justice Policy Review, 25*(2), 135–158.

National Highway Transportation Safety Administration. (2008, July). *Teen driver crashes: A report to Congress*. Washington, DC: U.S. Department of Transportation.

Quinn, P. D., & Harden, K. P. (2013). Behind the wheel and on the map: Genetic and environmental associations between drunk driving and other externalizing behaviors. *The Journal of Abnormal Psychology, 122*(4), 1166–1178.

Creating a Reference List in APA Style, Take-Home Assignment #1

Creating a Reference List for Your Paper

Create a reference list for your paper. Make sure that the list includes the minimum number of sources required by your instructor and that it is presented in APA style, consistent with the *Publication Manual* (6th edition). You must turn in the abstract for each source. *Failure to turn in the abstracts will result in a 2-point deduction per missing abstract.*

UNIT 8

Citing in the Text in APA Style

UNIT SUMMARY
Learning Objectives
Citing in the Text in APA Style: An Overview
Citing a Source at the End of a Sentence
    General Rules
    Citing One Author
    Citing Two Authors
    Citing Three, Four, or Five Authors
    Citing Six or More Authors
    Citing a Government Agency
    Citing Multiple Sources ("String" Citations)
        Sources With Only One Author
        Sources With Two, Three, Four, or Five Authors
        Sources With Six or More Authors
        Sources With an Author as a Single Author and as a Coauthor
        Sources With The Same Author, Published in Different Years
        Sources With The Same Author, Published in The Same Year
Incorporating a Citation Into a Sentence
    General Rules
    Citing One Author
        Citing the Same Source With One Author Within a Paragraph
        Citing the Same Source With One Author in Subsequent Paragraphs

Citing Two Authors
    Citing the Same Source With Two Authors Within a Paragraph
    Citing the Same Source With Two Authors in Subsequent Paragraphs
Citing Three, Four, or Five Authors
    Citing the Same Source With Three to Five Authors Within a Paragraph
    Citing the Same Source With Three to Five Authors in Subsequent Paragraphs
Citing Six or More Authors
    Citing the Same Source With Six or More Authors Within a Paragraph
    Citing the Same Source With Six or More Authors in Subsequent Paragraphs
Combining In-Sentence Citations With Citations at the Ends of Sentences
Miscellaneous Rules for Citing in the Text
    Citing a Secondary Source
    Incorporating a Quote Into a Sentence

Learning Objectives

At the end of this unit, students will be able to do the following:

- Cite sources in the text in APA style, in accordance with the *Publication Manual* (6th edition).

Citing in the Text in APA Style: An Overview

When you cite sources in the text of your paper, you must do so in APA style, in accordance with the *Publication Manual* (6th edition). This unit will teach you how to do that.

There are several important introductory facts and rules about citing sources in the text in APA style:

1. There are two purposes for citing sources in the text:
    a. to give credit to the author(s) of the information you have included in your paper, and
    b. to allow a reader to find sources by referring to your reference list.
2. You must cite all information that is not common knowledge. Common knowledge is knowledge that is familiar to most people, not just to you, your friends, or your professional peers.
3. Every source you cite in your paper must be included on your reference list and vice versa.
4. Every citation must contain the same basic information: the last name(s) of the author(s) and the year of publication.
5. There are three main ways to cite sources in the text:
    a. provide a citation at the end of the sentence,
    b. incorporate a citation into the sentence, or
    c. blend the two by citing at the end of some sentences and incorporating the citations into the text of others.

Citing a Source at the End of a Sentence

Although all of these are acceptable ways to cite, blending your citations is the preferred method because it adds variety to your paper and makes it flow more smoothly.

There are many APA rules about citing sources in the text. This unit will cover the basic rules that you are most likely to use when you write a paper. For additional rules about citing sources in the text, refer to the *Publication Manual* (6th edition) or www.apastyle.org/learn/index.aspx.

Citing a Source at the End of a Sentence

Placing a citation at the end of a sentence is the most basic way to cite a source. To do this, include the last name(s) of the author(s) and the year of publication within parentheses at the end of the sentence.

General Rules

When you cite a source at the end of a sentence, follow these rules:

- Write only the last name(s) of the author(s). Do not include first names or initials, and do not include a person's qualifications (e.g., JD, MD).
- When there are two or more authors of a source, list their names in the same order that they are listed in the original source. Never change the order of the authors.
- Place a period after the citation because it is part of the sentence.
- Include only the year of publication; do not include a month or season, even if one is given in the original source.
- When you place a citation at the end of a sentence, it means that everything you said *in that sentence* is attributable to that author. However, if you place the citation at the end of a paragraph, it means that *only that last sentence* is attributable to that author. In that situation, if any of the remaining sentences in the paragraph do not have citations, you will have committed plagiarism.

Citing One Author

When you cite one author, include the author's last name and the year of publication within parentheses. Place a comma between the name and the year of publication.

> **Example:**
>
> Most crimes are committed by males (Smith, 2016).

Every time you cite a single author at the end of a sentence, you must include both the last name and the year of publication.

Citing Two Authors

When you cite two authors, include the authors' last names and the year of publication within parentheses. Separate the names by an ampersand (&) and place a comma before the year of publication.

> **Example:**
>
> Boys commit more crimes than girls do (Smith & Jones, 2015).
>
> Note the following about the citation:
> - The authors' names are separated by an ampersand, not by the word "and."
> - There is no comma before the ampersand as there is when you cite multiple authors on a reference list.

Every time you cite two authors at the end of a sentence, you must include both names and the year of publication.

> **Example:**
>
> Boys commit more crimes than girls do (Smith & Jones, 2015). Most of the crimes they commit are misdemeanors (Otis & Harley, 2016).

This rule also applies when there is an intervening citation.

> **Example:**
>
> Boys commit more crimes than girls do (Smith & Jones, 2015). The majority of these crimes are misdemeanors (Otis & Harley, 2016). However, some boys do commit more serious crimes, such as assault and burglary (Smith & Jones, 2015).

Citing Three, Four, or Five Authors

When you cite three, four, or five authors, include the authors' last names and the year of publication within parentheses. Separate the names by commas, place a comma and then an ampersand before the last name, and place a comma before the date of publication.

> **Example:**
>
> Boys commit more crimes than girls do (Oakley, Wilson, & Jones, 2014).

The first time you cite three, four, or five authors in your paper, you must include all of the names, followed by the year of publication. Every subsequent time you cite that source in your paper, write the citation as (Oakley et al., 2014); et al. is a Latin abbreviation for *et alia*, which means *and others*. Note that there is no period after the *et* but there is one after the *al*. Note also that in the citation, there is no comma after Oakley but there is one before the year.

> **Example:**
>
> Boys commit more crimes than girls do (Oakley, Wilson, & Jones, 2014). However, most of the crimes they commit are misdemeanors (Oakley et al., 2014).

Citing a Source at the End of a Sentence

This rule also applies when there is an intervening citation.

Example:

Boys commit more crimes than girls do (Oakley, Wilson, & Jones, 2014). The majority of these crimes are misdemeanors (Otis & Harley, 2016). However, some boys do commit more serious crimes, such as assault and burglary (Oakley et al., 2014).

Citing Six or More Authors

When there are six or more authors, every time you cite that source, write only the first author's last name, followed by et al. and a comma, and then the year of publication.

Example:

Boys commit more crimes than girls do (Wilson et al., 2015).

Note! This is different from citing eight or more authors in the reference list, where you write the names of the first six authors followed by three ellipses points and then the final name.

Citing a Government Agency

When the author is a government agency, the first time you cite the source, write the name of the organization followed by the accepted abbreviation in brackets, then the year of publication. Every subsequent time you cite that source, write just the abbreviation and year of publication.

Example:

Juvenile drug courts provide many services to youth and their families (National Institute of Justice [NIJ], 2015). These services include counseling and education (NIJ, 2015).

Citing Multiple Sources ("String" Citations)

Sometimes you find the same information stated in several articles. To cite all of the sources, you must list the authors alphabetically by the first author and separate the sources by semicolons. After each author's name, write a comma and the year of publication.

Sources With Only One Author

When you write a string citation with sources by one author, list the authors alphabetically, not chronologically. Separate the sources by semicolons and do not use ampersands between them.

Example:

Most crimes are committed by males (Oakley, 2014; Smith, 2012; Wilson, 2013).

Note the following about this citation:

1. The names are listed alphabetically; do not get confused and list them chronologically.
2. The authors' names are separated by semicolons and there are no ampersands between them.

Sources With Two, Three, Four, or Five Authors

There are several rules to follow when you cite multiple authors in a string citation:

1. When a source has more than one author, alphabetize that source in the string citation by the first author's last name.
2. When a source has two authors, separate the names within the source by an ampersand.
3. When a source has three to five authors, separate the authors' names within the source by commas, and place an ampersand before the last author's name.

> **Example:**
>
> Men are more likely to drink and drive than women are (Carson, 2015; Clover & Otis, 2011; Jackson, Barnwell, & Halley, 2013).

4. When a source has three to five authors and you have already cited that source in your paper, you do not need to list all of the authors again. Instead, write the first author's name followed by et al., then a comma, and then the year of publication.

> **Example:**
>
> Young men between the ages of 18 and 21 are more likely to drink and drive than older men are (Carson, 2015; Clover & Otis, 2011; Jackson et al., 2012).

Sources With Six or More Authors

When a source has six or more authors, every time you cite the source, write only the first author's last name followed by et al., then a comma, and then the year of publication.

> **Example:**
>
> Men are more likely to drink and drive than women are (Carson et al., 2013; Clover & Otis, 2011; Jackson, Barnwell, & Halley, 2016; Parker, 2013).

Sources With an Author as a Single Author and as a Coauthor

If an author has published two articles, one with another author and one as the only author, cite first the article of which he or she is the sole author.

Example:

Men are more likely to drink and drive than women are (Clover, 2016; Clover & Otis, 2013).

Sources With the Same Author, Published in Different Years

If an author has published articles in different years, cite the oldest work first. Separate the years of publication by a comma.

Example:

Men are more likely to drink and drive than women are (Darnell, 2013, 2015).

Sources With the Same Author, Published in the Same Year

If an author has published more than one article in the same year, you must look at the titles of the sources to determine how to cite them. The source with the title that comes first alphabetically will be listed with an "a" following the year of publication. The source that comes second alphabetically will be listed with a "b" following the year of publication.

Example:

In 2014, L. P. Foster published two articles. The first is titled, "An Analysis of Recidivism Rates Associated With Juvenile Boot Camps." The second is titled, "An Evaluation of a Juvenile Boot Camp in Maryland." Alphabetically, "Analysis" comes before "Evaluation." Therefore, "An Analysis of Recidivism Rates Associated With Juvenile Boot Camps" would be cited in the text as (Foster, 2014a). "An Evaluation of a Juvenile Boot Camp in Maryland" would be cited in the text as (Foster, 2014b). If you cite both of those articles, the string citation would be as follows:

Boys who attend boot camps are less likely to recidivate than those who are placed in traditional juvenile facilities (Foster, 2014a, 2014b).

Incorporating a Citation Into a Sentence

Up to this point, we have discussed how to create a citation at the end of a sentence. Although it is an acceptable way to cite, citations at the end of every sentence makes your writing choppy and less interesting to read. Moreover, it is important that you use variety in your writing, because it will help your paper flow more smoothly. Accordingly, one way to remedy the choppiness associated with citing at the end of every sentence is to incorporate citations into the beginning of a sentence.

Example:

According to Oakley (2016), boys commit more crimes than girls do.
AND
Oakley (2016) found that boys commit more crimes than girls do.

General Rules

When you incorporate citations into a sentence, follow these rules:

- Write the name(s) of the author(s) immediately followed by the publication year within parentheses. Do not write the name(s) of the author(s) at the beginning of the sentence and the year at the end.

> **Example:**
>
> *Incorrect:* Johnson found similar results (2010).
> *Correct:* Johnson (2010) found similar results.

- Always include the year of publication within parentheses. Do not include it as part of the text of your sentence.

> **Example:**
>
> *Incorrect:* In 2013, Daniels found that DUI courts are successful in reducing recidivism.
> *Correct:* In a study, Daniels (2013) found that DUI courts are successful in reducing recidivism.

- Do not include the title of the article in the text.

> **Example:**
>
> *Incorrect:* In his article, "Raising Boys," Johnson (2015) found similar results.
> *Correct:* Johnson (2015) found similar results.

- If you have incorporated the citation into the sentence, do not also write it at the end of the sentence.

> **Example:**
>
> *Incorrect:* Johnson (2015) found similar results (2015).
> *Correct:* Johnson (2015) found similar results.

Citing One Author

When a source has one author, write the name as part of the text followed by the year of publication within parentheses.

Incorporating a Citation Into a Sentence

Example:

According to Daniels (2016), DUI courts are successful in reducing recidivism.

AND

Daniels (2016) found that DUI courts are successful in reducing recidivism.

Citing the Same Source With One Author Within a Paragraph

When you incorporate a citation into the beginning of a sentence, you can make your writing flow more smoothly by using some variety in the way you start each sentence. In particular, instead of starting every sentence with the author's name—for example, "According to Daniels (2016) . . ."— you can use pronouns.

Example:

According to Williams (2013), inmates who participate in parenting classes learn to show compassion for others. She further stated that they become more self-confident about their parenting skills. Therefore, she concluded that more prisons should offer these classes at their facilities.

If you use pronouns, there are several rules you must follow:

1. Write the author's name in the sentence that precedes the first sentence in which you use a pronoun.
2. Use pronouns only when you cite the same source in *the same paragraph*.
3. If you use a pronoun, use the correct gender for the author.
4. After you have cited the author's name and year of publication, if you use his or her name again instead of a pronoun, do not include the year in subsequent citations in that paragraph.

Example:

According to Williams (2013), inmates who participate in parenting classes learn to show compassion for others. She further stated that they become more self-confident about their parenting skills. Therefore, Williams concluded that more prisons should offer these classes at their facilities.

5. If there is an intervening citation between your citations to Williams, you must write her name again, and you must include the year of publication in the citation.

Example:

According to Williams (2013), inmates who participate in parenting classes learn to show compassion for others. Wilson (2016) similarly found that the inmates become more self-confident about their parenting skills. Therefore, Williams (2013) concluded that more prisons should offer these classes at their facilities.

Citing the Same Source With One Author in Subsequent Paragraphs

When you cite a source in subsequent paragraphs, you must include the year again the first time you cite the source in the new paragraph. For subsequent citations to that source within that paragraph, the same rules apply that were previously discussed.

Citing Two Authors

When you cite two authors in the text of your sentence, separate their names with the word "and." This is different than when you cite at the end of a sentence and use an ampersand between the authors' names. After the second author's name, write the date of publication within parentheses.

> **Example:**
>
> According to Wilson and Black (2015), there are many benefits to prison education programs.
> *AND*
> Wilson and Black (2015) found that there are many benefits to prison education programs.

Citing the Same Source With Two Authors Within a Paragraph

You can make your paper flow more smoothly by using the pronoun "they" when you cite the same source with two authors.

> **Example:**
>
> Wilson and Black (2015) found that there are many benefits to prison education programs. In particular, they found that inmates who successfully complete a GED program are more likely to find employment when they are released. They found similar results for inmates who participate in vocational training classes.

If you use pronouns, there are several rules you must follow:

- Write the authors' names in the sentence that precedes the first sentence in which you use a pronoun.
- Use pronouns only when you cite the source by the same authors in *the same paragraph*.
- After you have cited the authors' names and year of publication, if you use their names again instead of a pronoun, do not include the year in subsequent citations in that paragraph.

> **Example:**
>
> Wilson and Black (2015) found that there are many benefits to prison education programs. In particular, they found that inmates who successfully complete a GED program are more likely to find employment when they are released. Wilson and Black found similar results for inmates who participate in vocational training classes.

Incorporating a Citation Into a Sentence

- If there is an intervening citation, include the authors' names and the year of publication in the next citation to that source.

> **Example:**
>
> Wilson and Black (2015) found that there are many benefits to prison education programs. According to Clover and Otis (2014), inmates who successfully complete a GED program are more likely to find employment when they are released. Wilson and Black (2015) found similar results for inmates who participate in vocational training classes.

Citing the Same Source With Two Authors in Subsequent Paragraphs

When you cite a source with the same two authors in subsequent paragraphs, you must include the year the first time you cite the source. For subsequent citations to that source within that paragraph, the same rules that were previously discussed apply.

Citing Three, Four, or Five Authors

When you cite three, four, or five authors, separate the next-to-last author's and the last author's names with the word *and*. In addition, include a comma before the *and*. Then write the publication year within parentheses.

> **Example:**
>
> According to Oakley, Wilson, and Clover (2016), youth who are abused or neglected are more likely to commit crimes as adults.

The first time you cite three, four, or five authors in your paper, you must include all of the names. Every subsequent time you cite that source in your paper, write the citation as Oakley et al. (2016).

Citing the Same Source With Three to Five Authors Within a Paragraph

After you have written the full citation in a paragraph, if you cite Oakley et al. again in that paragraph and there are no intervening citations, you do not need to put the year of publication.

> **Example:**
>
> According to Oakley, Wilson, and Clover (2016), boys commit more crimes than girls do. However, Oakley et al. have found that most of the crimes they commit are misdemeanors.

When your source has three to five authors, you can also use the pronoun "they" to make your paper flow more smoothly. Follow the same rules discussed in the section about using "they" when citing a source with the same two authors.

Example:

According to Oakley, Wilson, and Clover (2016), boys commit more crimes than girls do. However, they have found that most of the crimes they commit are misdemeanors.

If there is an intervening citation in a paragraph between two Oakley citations, you must put the first author's name followed by et al., and the publication year within parentheses in the next citation to that source.

Example:

According to Oakley, Wilson, and Clover (2016), boys commit more crimes than girls do. However, Otis (2014) found that most of the crimes they commit are misdemeanors. Further, Oakley et al. (2016) found that some boys do commit more serious crimes, such as assault and burglary.

Citing the Same Source With Three to Five Authors in Subsequent Paragraphs

When you cite the same source with three to five authors in subsequent paragraphs, you must include the year the first time you cite the source. Remember, you do not need to write out all of the authors' names; write the citation as Oakley et al. (2016). For subsequent citations to that source within that paragraph, the same rules that were previously discussed apply.

Citing Six or More Authors

When you cite six or more authors in the text, write just the first author's last name followed by et al. and then the year of publication within parentheses.

Example:

According to Oakley et al. (2014), boys commit more crimes than girls do.

Citing the Same Source With Six or More Authors Within a Paragraph

Once you have given the full citation, you do not need to include the year again in that same paragraph.

When your source has six or more authors, you can use the pronoun "they" to make your paper flow more smoothly. Follow the same rules discussed in the section about using "they" when citing a source with the same two authors.

Example:

According to Wilson et al. (2011), boys commit more crimes than girls do. However, they have found that most of the crimes they commit are misdemeanors.

Combining In-Sentence Citations With Citations at the Ends of Sentences

If there is an intervening citation in that paragraph, include the first author's name followed by et al. and the year of publication within parentheses in the second citation to that source.

Example:

According to Wilson et al. (2011), boys commit more crimes than girls do. However, Clover (2011) found that most of the crimes they commit are misdemeanors. Further, Wilson et al. (2011) found that some boys do commit more serious crimes, such as assault and burglary.

Citing the Same Source With Six or More Authors in Subsequent Paragraphs

When you cite those authors in subsequent paragraphs, include the year the first time you cite that source. For subsequent citations to that source within that paragraph, the same rules apply that were previously discussed.

Combining In-Sentence Citations With Citations at the Ends of Sentences

When you write your paper, the best way to cite your sources is by using a combination of in-sentence citations and citations at the ends of your sentences. By using variety in the way you cite, your paper will flow more smoothly and will be more interesting for the reader.

You can combine in-sentence citations with citations at the ends of sentences in different ways:

- Write some citations at the ends of your sentences and some as part of your text.

Example:

Researchers have found that boys commit more crimes than girls do (Oakley, Wilson, & Clover, 2011). Specifically, White and Johnson (2015) found that most of the crimes boys commit are misdemeanors. However, further research has revealed that some boys do commit more serious crimes, such as assault and burglary (Charles, Baldwin, & Cooper, 2016).

- Include string citations at the ends of some sentences, and incorporate citations into the beginnings of other sentences.

Example:

Researchers have found that boys commit more crimes than girls do (Adams, 2015; Oakley, Wilson, & Clover, 2011). Specifically, Oakley et al. found that most of the crimes boys commit are misdemeanors. However, further research has revealed that some boys do commit more serious crimes, such as assault and burglary (Adams, 2015).

Note! In this example, you do not need a year following "Oakley et al." because there are no intervening citations between it and the full citation. However, you do need to include a year for the Adams citation because you must always cite the year when you include a parenthetical citation at the end of a sentence.

Miscellaneous Rules for Citing in the Text

There are important miscellaneous rules to follow when you cite in the text.

Citing a Secondary Source

Often an author will state a proposition in his or her article and then cite the source from which he or she got that information.

> **Example:**
>
> You are reading an article written by Moore (2015). In it, Moore writes, "Youths from single-parent homes are more likely to become truant (Yardley, 2010)."

Here, Yardley is the primary source and Moore is the secondary source. When you want to use that information in your paper, locate and read Yardley's article and then cite it in the text and on your reference list. However, it is not always possible to obtain an original source. If you are unable to locate the original source, cite Moore in the text and on your reference list (because that is the source you actually read) and refer to Yardley's article in your text.

> **Example:**
>
> Yardley (2010) found youths from single-parent homes are more likely to become truant (as cited in Moore, 2015).

Incorporating a Quote Into a Sentence

When you cite a direct quote, include the name(s) of the author(s) and the page(s) from which you got the quote. There are two ways you can incorporate a quote into a sentence:

1. Write the name(s) of the author(s) and the year of publication as part of your text and then write the page number(s) within parentheses after the quoted material. Place a period after the parentheses.

> **Example:**
>
> Oakley and Wilson (2012) found that "violent offenders are four times more likely to recidivate than non-violent offenders" (p. 273).

2. Write the name(s) of the author(s) and the year of publication at the end of your sentence within parentheses. Include the page number(s) in the parentheses. Place a period after the parentheses.

> **Example:**
>
> "Violent offenders are more likely to recidivate than nonviolent offenders" (Oakley & Wilson, 2012, p. 23).

Miscellaneous Rules for Citing in the Text

> *See the following handouts at the end of this unit:*
> ***Citing in the Text in APA Style, Class Exercise #1:** "Identifying Errors According to APA Style for Citing in the Text"*
> ***Citing in the Text in APA Style, Class Exercise #2:** "Identifying Real-Life Errors According to APA Style for Citing in the Text"*
> ***Citing in the Text in APA Style, Handout #1:** "Reference Guide"*
> ***Citing in the Text in APA Style, Handout #2:** "APA Citing in the Text: A Real-Life Example"*

NOTES

Citing in the Text in APA Style, Class Exercise #1

Identifying Errors According to APA Style for Citing in the Text, Part I

Read the following sentences and determine whether the underlined citations are correctly written according to APA style. If they are correct, write correct *above them. If they are incorrect, rewrite them so they are correct.*

1. There are many problems with boot camps (J. Knowles, 2012).

2. Juvenile drug use is increasing in the United States (Oakley, Smith & Jones, 2015).

3. Miller conducted a study that examined whether boys from single-parent homes are more likely to commit crimes than boys who are raised in homes with two parents (2013).

4. In his study, Sternberg, (2010) discussed how the social learning theory related to juvenile violence. In the study, Sternberg (2010) also briefly discussed the social control theory.

5. Garcia & Smith (2016) found that elder abuse is common in nursing homes. Garcia et al. also found that most of the abuse is committed by staff members.

6. Basil, Williams, Clover, Daniels, Robertson, Edwards, and Smith (2015) found that children who are abused are more likely to abuse their own children.

7. Kelly, Stark, and Bert (2010) found that 7% of teenagers drank alcohol and then drove. In another study, Gamble and Clark found that 85% of all automobile accidents involving teenagers also involved alcohol. Based on these studies, Kelly, Stark, and Bert concluded that programs must be developed to address the problem of teenagers who drink and drive.

8. One example of an alternative sanction for juveniles is boot camps (Neal, 2015; Little & Johns, 2012).

9. Punishment is the foundation of the deterrence theory (Smith, 2015; Lucky and Oliver, 2011; Smith & Travis, 2015).

Citing in the Text in APA Style, Class Exercise #1

Identifying Errors According to APA Style for Citing in the Text, Part II

Rewrite the following sentences using correct citations:

1. In an article published in 2014, Smith found that the number of juveniles sentenced to boot camps has decreased.

   _____

   _____

   _____

2. Boys are more likely to skip school than girls are (Smith, 2015). In addition, boys are more likely to stay out past midnight (Smith, 2015). Finally, boys are more likely to smoke cigarettes than girls are (Smith, 2015).

   _____

   _____

   _____

Citing in the Text in APA Style, Class Exercise #2

Identifying Real-Life Errors According to APA Style for Citing in the Text

Read the following paragraphs and determine whether the citations are correctly written. If a citation is correct as written, write correct *above it. If it is incorrect, revise it to be correct. If a citation is included where it should not be included, make a mark through it. Finally, if a citation is missing, note where it should be included.*

The following material has been modified from Ferree, C. W. (2006). *DUI recidivism and attorney type: Is there a connection?* (Unpublished master's thesis). School of Criminal Justice, University of Baltimore, Baltimore, MD.

1. Each year, millions of indigent defendants rely on publicly appointed counsel for legal representation, and each year, enormous sums of money are spent on their defense. For example, according to DeFrances & Litras (2000), in 1999, public counsel represented indigent offenders in approximately 4.2 million cases (DeFrances & Litras). Moreover, that same year, taxpayers spent an estimated $1.2 billion on indigent legal defense in the 100 most populous counties in the United States.

2. In order to decrease recidivism rates, courts have imposed various sanctions on offenders (James, Walker, Smith, Jones, Tyler, & Baker)(2001). Historically, individuals who were convicted of alcohol-impaired driving were punished through incarceration (Lucker and Osti, 1997). They stated that this approach was based on a deterrence theory under which policymakers believed that fewer individuals would drink and drive if they faced swift, certain, and severe punishments. In accordance with this policy, as of 1988, 42 states had adopted laws mandating incarceration for repeat DWI offenders (Martin, Annan, & Forst, 1993; Lucker & Osti, 1997). In addition, 14 states had passed laws mandating jail sentences for first-time DWI offenders (Lucker et al., 1997).

The following three paragraphs go together as an excerpt from a paper. For this section, if a citation is correct as written, write correct *above it. If it is incorrect, rewrite it correctly. If a citation is included where it should not be included, make a mark through it. Finally, if a citation is missing, note where it should be included.*

3. According to Neinstadt, Zatz, and Epperlein (1998), of the millions of defendants who use appointed counsel, many defendants share similar characteristics. In particular, indigent defendants are likely to be either unemployed or employed part time, and are typically from a lower socioeconomic class (Champion, 1989; Nienstadt, Zatz, & Epperlein, 1998; Sterling, 1983; Baker and Jones, 2000). They are also likely to have prior criminal records, be young, and have low levels of education (Sterling, 1983).

Citing in the Text in APA Style, Class Exercise #2

In addition to the similarities among the personal characteristics of indigent defendants, studies have found similarities in the crimes with which they are charged. According to Neinstadt, Zatz, & Epperlein, in state courts, indigent defendants who are represented by public attorneys are more likely to be charged with serious crimes (e.g., violent crimes, property offenses, and drug crimes) (1998). In contrast, Harlow (2000) found that offenders who are represented by private attorneys are more likely to be charged with less serious crimes, such as public order offenses (including driving offenses) (Harlow, 2000).

Studies have also shown that offenders who hire private attorneys share certain characteristics (Baker & Jones, 2000). In particular, in 1983, Sterling found that defendants who are represented by private counsel are more likely to be charged with narcotics offenses than with more serious felonies such as robbery or burglary. It was also found that those offenders were less likely to have a prior record, or to have been out on bail, probation, or parole at the time of the commission of the offense.

Citing in the Text in APA Style, Handout #1

Reference Guide
End-of-Sentence Citations
One author: (Smith, 2012).
Two authors: (Smith & Jones, 2012).
Three to five authors:
> First time: (Oakley, Wilson, & Jones, 2012).
> Every subsequent time: (Oakley et al., 2012).

Six or more authors (every time): (Wilson et al., 2014).
Government agency as author:
> First time: (National Institute of Health [NIH], 2014).
> Every subsequent time: (NIH, 2014).

Several sources, same information (alphabetical by first author's last name):
> (Oakley & Smith, 2014; Smith & Jones, 2016).
> (Oakley, 2013; Smith, 2014; Wilson, Edwards, & Jones, 2015).
> (Oakley, 2013; Smith, 2014; Smith & Brown, 2015).

Same author, different years: (Smith, 2011, 2014).
Same author in same year (alphabetical by article title in the reference list):
> "An Analysis of . . ." In the reference list—Smith, J. C. (2015a). In the text—(Smith, 2015a)
> "An Evaluation of . . ." In the reference list—Smith, J. C. (2015b). In the text—(Smith, 2015b)

In-Text Citations
One author: According to Smith (2014) . . . (*not*, "In 2014, Smith found . . .")
Two authors: In contrast, Smith and Jones (2013) argued that . . . They also found . . .
Three to five authors:
> First time: According to Smith, Jones, Walker, and Gable (2015) . . .
> Every subsequent time: Furthermore, Smith et al. (2015) noted . . .

Six or more authors (every time): According to Adams et al. (2013) . . .

Rule: Once you introduce another source, you must give a full citation: Source A → Source B → Source A.

Example:
According to Oakley, Wilson, and Clover (2011), boys commit more crimes than girls do. However, Otis (2011) found that most of the crimes they commit are misdemeanors. Further, Oakley et al. (2011) found that some boys do commit more serious crimes, such as assault and burglary.

Citing in the Text in APA Style, Handout #2

APA Citing in the Text: A Real-Life Example

The following material has been modified from Ferree, C. W. (2006). *DUI recidivism and attorney type: Is there a connection?* (Unpublished master's thesis). School of Criminal Justice, University of Baltimore, Baltimore, MD.

Over the past several decades, alcohol-impaired driving has become a very serious problem in the United States. According to the Centers for Disease Control and Prevention (CDCP, 2004), in 2002, 1.5 million people were arrested for driving while impaired. Moreover, studies have shown that alcohol-related automobile accidents are a leading cause of death and physical injury (Marzano, 2004; Meyer & Gray, 1997; National Highway Traffic Safety Administration [NHTSA], 2005). It is estimated that, each year, 120 million people drink and drive, although the exact number is difficult to determine because many people drink and drive but are never caught (Marzano, 2004; Voas & Fisher, 2001). In fact, Breer, Schwartz, Schillo, and Savage (2003) estimated that individuals might drive 1,000 times while under the influence of alcohol before they are stopped by the police.

Although driving under the influence of alcohol is one of the greatest public safety concerns in the United States, Voas and Fisher (2001) report that the number of alcohol-related traffic fatalities has decreased by approximately 20% over the past 20 years. Similarly, Breer et al. (2003) found that from 1993 through 2003, the number of individuals who drove while intoxicated also decreased. Despite this decrease, alcohol-related accidents occur across the United States at a staggering rate. According to the CDCP (2004), someone is killed in an alcohol-related automobile accident every 31 minutes, and someone is injured in such an accident every 2 minutes. The CDCP also found that, every year, 40% of all traffic-related deaths are alcohol-related. In total, in 2003 and 2004, approximately 17,000 people were killed as a result of alcohol-related driving accidents (NHTSA, 2005).

UNIT 9

Preparing for the Job Market

UNIT SUMMARY
Learning Objectives
Writing a Résumé: An Overview
Writing a Résumé: The Basic Rules About Appearance
Writing a Résumé: The Basic Rules About Content
Writing a Résumé: Getting Started
- Education Information
- Employment Information
- Certifications and Technological Skills
- Academic and Professional Honors
- Community and Professional Engagement

Writing a Résumé: The Details
- The Appearance
- The Specific Sections
    - Contact Information
    - The Objective
    - Education
    - Related Experience
    - Employment History
    - Certifications and Technological Skills
    - Academic and Professional Honors
    - Community and Professional Engagement
    - References

Writing a Cover Letter: An Overview
    The Importance of Writing a Good Cover Letter
    Specific Tips to Follow When Writing a Cover Letter
Electronic Communications: An Overview
    Tips for Drafting a Professional Email
Professional Social Media Profiles: An Overview
    The Negative Impact of an Unprofessional Social Media Profile
    Creating a Professional Social Media Profile
        LinkedIn: An Overview
            Creating a LinkedIn Profile

Learning Objectives

At the end of this unit, students will be able to do the following:

- Write a chronological résumé.
- Write a cover letter.
- Draft a professional email.
- Identify negative elements employers look for in a social media profile.
- Create a professional social media profile on LinkedIn.

Writing a Résumé: An Overview

The first step in the hiring process is to provide a prospective employer with a résumé. Because the résumé will be the first impression you make, you must be sure that it is well organized, error free, and succinct. Employers typically receive dozens, if not hundreds, of résumés for a single job opening and have only a limited amount of time to spend reviewing each one. Thus, you should make your résumé as concise as possible, highlighting your accomplishments in an easy-to-read and professional format.

When you write your résumé, it is imperative that you use correct spelling and proper grammar. Employers who receive résumés with spelling and grammar errors typically assume that you will make similar mistakes at work, and they will reject your application.

Note! Many students erroneously believe that the purpose of a résumé is to get a job. It is not. The purpose of a résumé is to get an interview, so that you can discuss in person, with your prospective employer, your qualifications for the job.

There are many different types of résumés. In this unit, you will learn how to write a chronological résumé. When you write this type of résumé, you list your most recent accomplishments first and end with your former accomplishments. In addition, you organize your information into the following categories: *Education, Related Experience, Employment History, Certifications* and *Technological Skills, Academic and Professional Honors,* and *Community and Professional Engagement*. Exclude any category in which you do not have experience.

Writing a Résumé: The Basic Rules About Appearance

One of the most important things to remember when you write a résumé is that it must have a professional appearance. Accordingly, follow these basic rules:

- Use a traditional font that is easy to read (e.g., Arial, Times New Roman). Do not use a flowery, "pretty" font in an attempt to make your résumé stand out from the others. Doing so does not impress the employer and only serves to detract from the professionalism of your résumé.
- With the exception of the font you use for your name, use the same font size throughout your résumé (10 pt.–14 pt. font size). Make your name one font size larger than the font size you select for the rest of the résumé.
- Use heavy bond in a neutral-colored paper such as linen or off-white. Do not use a "pretty" color in the hopes that it will stand out from the other résumés or to impress your reader. The purpose of a résumé is not to be creative or artful; it is to present your qualifications in a professional manner.
- Limit your résumé to one or two pages. A prospective employer does not have time to read a long, elaborate résumé. At the interview, you will be able to discuss in detail your qualifications and experiences.

Writing a Résumé: The Basic Rules About Content

The content of your résumé must be well written and presented in a succinct, professional manner. To ensure you do this, follow these guidelines:

- Include only the information that you feel makes you a strong candidate for the position and that you feel would impress an employer. For example, include information about a job in which you were given supervisory duties, but do not include a job if you held it for only a few weeks.
- When you write your résumé, use spell check. However, remember that it will not catch all errors, such as when you use the wrong homophone.
- Tailor your résumé so that it is geared toward the position for which you are applying.

> **Example:**
>
> An individual has experience both in corrections and in store security. If that person applies for a job in corrections, she should emphasize her experience in corrections and any education or training she has received that is related to corrections. In contrast, if she is applying for a job in store security, she should emphasize her education and experiences that are related to security.

In addition to the rules governing what you should include in your résumé, there are also rules about what you should *not* include:

- Your marital status, age, or any other information that is irrelevant to procuring the job.
- Your salary requirements. If the employer wants to know that information, he or she can discuss it with you during your interview.

- Handwritten changes to your résumé after you have printed it out. If you see that there is a mistake on it and you do not have time to retype it before you give it to the employer, leave it as it is. Correcting a mistake in ink will only draw attention to it.

Writing a Résumé: Getting Started

When you write a basic chronological résumé, you will present your information in six sections. Therefore, the first thing you should do is make a list of the sections you will include. These are: *Education Information, Related Experience, Employment History, Certifications and Technological Skills, Academic and Professional Honors,* and *Community and Professional Engagement*. List the sections in the same order in which they will appear in your résumé. Once you have made your list, write all of the information you want to include in each of those sections. After you have written that information, you will edit and organize it into the format discussed in this unit.

Education Information

For this section, list the academic institutions you attended after graduating from high school. These include trade schools, community colleges, and four-year colleges or universities that you attended or from which you graduated. For each school, write the name, location (city and state), and year(s) you attended.

If you attended a school for less than a year, write the months and year that you attended the school. If you are in the process of receiving a degree from a school, write your expected date of graduation. If you have received a degree from any of the schools you listed, write the name of the degree and your discipline of study (e.g., Bachelor of Science in Criminology), and the date on which you received your degree. If you graduated with honors or with any other distinction (e.g., cum laude), include that information as well. Do not, however, include your GPA. The employer can verify that information from your transcripts if it is pertinent.

Employment Information

For this section, list all of the jobs you have held since high school graduation. Include all part-time and full-time jobs, as well as internships (paid and unpaid) that you have held. If you have been out of high school for more than 10 years, list only the jobs you have held within the past 10 years. For each job, write the name of the business, the city and state where it is located, the dates you were employed, your job title, and your job duties. If you did not have an official job title, create one that best describes your position.

Certifications and Technological Skills

For this section, list the certifications or special training you have received, as well as technological (e.g., computer-related) skills you have that are related to the job you are seeking. For example, if you are applying for a law enforcement position and you have received training in firearms, you would include that on your list. In this section, you should also list any foreign languages in which you are proficient.

When you list your computer-related skills, highlight only those computer programs in which you are proficient that would require additional training to master, such as statistical packages (e.g., SPSS, GIS, CrimeStat) or specialized databases (e.g., LexisNexis, NCIC). Do not include programs that most employers assume candidates would be proficient in (e.g., Word, PowerPoint).

Academic and Professional Honors

For this section, list all of the academic and professional honors you have received since you graduated from high school. Examples of honors you would list are awards (or recognition)

Writing a Résumé: The Details

you received from a school or organization, such as making the dean's list or winning an academic award.

> **Example:**
> Write some examples of honors you have received that you could include in your résumé.
> _____
> _____

Community and Professional Engagement

For this final section, include all activities that reflect your contribution to your community and profession. Examples of activities you would list include volunteer jobs (e.g., American Red Cross blood drive), memberships in national and local professional organizations (e.g., Academy of Criminal Justice Sciences), and memberships in any school clubs that are related to your discipline.

> **Example:**
> Write some examples of community and professional activities you engage in, or have engaged in, that you could include in your résumé.
> _____
> _____

Writing a Résumé: The Details

You must follow certain rules to ensure that your résumé is presented professionally, because its appearance is the first impression you will make on a prospective employer. To help you better understand how to present a professional-looking résumé, this section discusses the sample résumé located at the end of this unit.

> See **Preparing for the Job Market, Handout #1: "Sample Résumé"** at the end of this unit.

The Appearance

There are certain things you should note about the overall appearance of the sample résumé:

- The name is typed in bold, in a font size that is larger than the font size used in the rest of the résumé.
- Each heading is capitalized and in bold font (e.g., **OBJECTIVE**, **EDUCATION**). This gives the résumé an organized appearance and allows the employer to find sections quickly and with minimal effort.
- The dates relating to education and work experience are set apart from the written content. This makes it easier for the employer to glance through a résumé and see the dates relating to your education and your job experience.

- All of the information included within each category is presented in succinct phrases. There are no periods at the end of the phrases.
- Each job duty, certification, technological skill, honor, and community and professional engagement activity is set in a bulleted list. This makes it easy for the prospective employer to quickly read them.
- The résumé is double-spaced between the categories and between each entry in a category. However, the entries are single-spaced.
- All of the information for the **RELATED EXPERIENCE** section fits onto the first page. However, you may find that information in this section (or another section) must be split over two pages. If this is the case, do not break entries; insert a page break so the entire entry appears on the second page.

Example:

On the sample résumé, if all of the information for the Best Buy job had not fit onto the first page, Jane Doe would have inserted a page break directly after the previous job description—Nordstrom—so that the entire Best Buy section would appear on the second page.

The Specific Sections

As well as having a professional appearance, your résumé must include specific information. Before listing the six categories discussed previously, your résumé will begin with your Contact Information and your Objective.

Contact Information

There are several things you should note about the Contact Information in the sample résumé:

- The Contact Information is centered at the top of the résumé. Only your name should be in bold type, and one font size larger than the rest of the Contact Information. Do *not* write your name in capital letters.
- The email address is professional, *not* creative or clever. If you do not have a professional email address, you should create one.
- There is one telephone number; this should be the number that will allow the employer to easily contact you.

Note! If you can be easily reached at several numbers, include them all on your résumé. Beside each number, indicate the type of telephone number (e.g., cell, work, home). If you have a preference for which number you would like the employer to use to contact you, be sure to note it by typing "preferred" next to that telephone number.

Example:

Jane L. Doe
236 Main Street
Baltimore, MD 21209
(410) 333-5609
jdoe@gmail.com

Writing a Résumé: The Details

The Objective

The Objective sets the tone for your résumé. Its purpose is to allow you to briefly tell the employer what you will bring to the job. You should make the Objective job specific and succinct.

When you write your Objective, think about the position you are seeking and any special skills or interests you have that would strengthen your qualifications for that position. Often, it is helpful to refer back to the position advertisement when you write your Objective. Specifically, when you describe yourself in your Objective, you can use the adjectives that have been specified as necessary or desirable for the potential candidate to have.

> **Example:**
>
> The job posting states, "Seeking self-directed individual with experience working with children, to provide daily in-class assistance to special needs youth."
>
> You can write that you are a hard-working, motivated student with early childhood education experience.

> **Example:**
>
> **OBJECTIVE**
>
> Highly motivated and dependable Bachelor's candidate seeking full-time position in federal law enforcement. More than six years of security and management experience in the private sector, certified as an Emergency Response Coordinator by the American Red Cross, and certified by the International Foundation of Protection Officers.

Note! In the sample résumé, the Objective is very short and does not include full sentences. Moreover, it briefly highlights the applicant's attributes (e.g., current education level, position sought, length of related work experience, and relevant certification).

Education

In this section, you should include all of your postsecondary education information, starting with the most recent. You should include information about all of the schools you attended: those from which you received a degree, those from which you are in the process of receiving a degree, and those you attended but from which you did not receive a degree.

For each degree you have earned, in italics, write the title of the degree and discipline in which you received it, followed by a comma and the year you received it, also in italics. Below that, in regular font, write the full name of the school you attended, and the city and state where it is located. When you write the state's abbreviation, write it in capital letters and do not include periods. If you graduated with honors from a school, include that information.

Example:

If you earned a degree, follow this format:
EDUCATION
Bachelor of Science in Criminal Justice, 2015
Roanoke College, Roanoke, VA
- Graduated with honors

If you are in the process of earning a degree, write the title of the degree and discipline in which you will receive it in italics, followed by a comma. Below that, in regular font, write the full name of the school you attend and the city and state where it is located. To the right, write the date you expect to receive your diploma so that it is on the same line as the degree you will earn and insert a right margin tab so that it is flush with the right margin.

Example:

If you are in the process of earning a degree, follow this format for the date:
EDUCATION
Bachelor of Science in Criminology,   Expected in May 2018
University of Baltimore, Baltimore, MD

If you attended a school but did not graduate from it, list the name of the school, its location, and the years you attended. If you attended the school for less than one year, include the months and year you attended. If you attended more than one school from which you did not graduate, list each one.

Example:

If you attended an institution but do not anticipate graduating from that school, provide dates you attended:
EDUCATION
Bucknell University, Lewisburg, PA   January 2014–June 2015

Related Experience

In this category, starting with your most recent job, list your work experience in fields that are related to the job you are seeking.

Note! If you have not had any experience in a related field, you will not include a Related Experience section. Instead, you will list all of your work experience in your Employment History, which will be discussed in the next section.

Your Related Experience includes all full-time work, part-time work, and internships (paid or unpaid). For each job you held (or currently hold), list the name of the company in capital letters. Following that, in lowercase letters, write the name of the city and, in capital letters, write the abbreviation for the state where you work(ed). To the right, insert a right margin tab and write the dates of your employment so they are flush with the right margin.

Beneath the name of the company, in bold font, write your job title. If you did not have an official title, create one that best describes your position. Beneath that, using bullets, write *short* phrases stating your most important job duties. Always list at least two duties, but do not list more than five. In addition, do not write lengthy explanations for what you did, and do not write *etc*. You can explain your job duties in more detail during your interview with your prospective employer.

When you state your job duties at your current job, write your verbs in the present tense (e.g., supervise 25 employees). When you describe the job duties you performed in a past job, write your verbs in the past tense (e.g., prepared theft reports).

When you state your job duties, use forceful verbs and write objectively; do not sing your own praises. If you wrote well or performed your job well, that will be reflected in your references.

Example:

Do not say: Was responsible for preparing well-written and thorough theft reports for management.

Instead, simply say: Prepared theft reports for management.

Example:

RELATED EXPERIENCE

NORDSTROM—Tysons Corner, VA   April 2010–present

Manager of Loss Prevention Operations

- Supervise 25 employees
- Hire and train all new employees
- Facilitate and consult with corporate headquarters in the development and implementation of new security protocols
- Oversee all investigations

NORDSTROM—Tysons Corner, VA   March 2009–April 2010

Loss Prevention Specialist

- Prepared theft reports for management
- Assisted manager with employee training and loss prevention
- Created new security protocol for prevention of employee theft

BEST BUY—Towson, MD   February 2007–March 2009

Loss Prevention Specialist

- Assisted manager in investigating in-store thefts
- Prepared loss reports

Employment History

Present your past and current employment information in the same way that you presented your Related Experience information; however, in this section, include all work experience you have had that is *not* related to the job you are seeking. If all of your work experience is related to the job you are seeking, you will not include this section.

Again, you should include all full-time work, part-time work, and internships (paid or unpaid), beginning with the most recent.

Example:

EMPLOYMENT HISTORY

REI—Timonium, MD   June 2006–January 2007

Sales Representative

- Assisted customers
- Organized and catalogued inventory
- Assisted manager in training new employees

PIZZA HUT—Towson, MD   October 2005–June 2006

Head Hostess

- Supervised waitstaff
- Trained all new front-staff employees
- Assisted manager with payroll

Note! In the sample résumé, all of Jane Doe's most recent jobs were related to the one she was seeking, and the older ones were not. However, it is possible that your work experience may go back and forth between the two categories so that the correct chronological order is split between the two. This is acceptable.

Example:

RELATED EXPERIENCE

NORDSTROM—Tysons Corner, VA   April 2010–present

Manager of Loss Prevention Operations

- Supervise 25 employees
- Hire and train all new employees
- Facilitate and consult with corporate headquarters in the development and implementation of new security protocols
- Oversee all investigations

BEST BUY—Towson, MD   February 2007–March 2009

Loss Prevention Specialist

- Assisted manager in investigating in-store thefts
- Prepared loss reports

Example: *(continued)*

NORDSTROM—Towson, MD   June 2006–January 2007
Loss Prevention Specialist

- Prepared theft reports for management
- Assisted manager with employee training and loss prevention
- Created new security protocol for prevention of employee theft

EMPLOYMENT HISTORY

REI—Timonium, MD   March 2009–April 2010
Sales Representative

- Assisted customers
- Organized and catalogued inventory
- Assisted manager in training new employees

PIZZA HUT—Towson, MD   October 2005–June 2006
Head Hostess

- Supervised waitstaff
- Trained all new front-staff employees
- Assisted manager with payroll

Certifications and Technological Skills

In this section, list your certifications and technological (computer) skills in regular font and in short, bulleted phrases. Also list any foreign languages in which you are proficient. Remember, list only the computer skills that required additional training; do not list basic computer skills.

Example:

CERTIFICATIONS AND TECHNOLOGICAL SKILLS

- Completed the Certified Protection Officer Program (CPO) through the International Foundation of Protection Officers, June 2010. Recertified: June 2012, June 2014
- Certified as Emergency Response Coordinator through Red Cross of America, June 2009
- Proficient in GIS, SPSS, LexisNexis

Academic and Professional Honors

In this section, include all of the academic and professional honors you have received since you graduated from high school. For each honor you list, first write the honor in regular font. Then write the name of the institution from which you received that honor. Beneath that, also in regular font and using bullets, list the relevant dates, starting with the most recent one.

Example:

ACADEMIC AND PROFESSIONAL HONORS

Dean's List—University of Baltimore

- Spring 2016, Fall 2015

Community and Professional Engagement

In this section, list the activities that indicate your contribution to your community and profession. The format of these entries is similar to that used in the Academic and Professional Honors section. In addition, if you held (or hold) a position in an organization, write the name of the position in italics followed by a comma and then the relevant dates (in regular font).

> **Example:**
>
> **COMMUNITY AND PROFESSIONAL ENGAGEMENT**
>
> Red Cross of America
> - *Volunteer*, 2009 to present
>
> Academy of Criminal Justice Sciences
> - *Member*, Fall 2010 to present
>
> International Association of Professional Security Consultants
> - *Member*, 2013 to present
>
> Criminal Justice Student Association
> University of Baltimore, Baltimore, MD
> - *Member*, Fall 2010 to Spring 2013
> - *Officer (Secretary)*, Spring 2011 to Spring 2013

References

The last thing you should include on your résumé is the brief statement, "References available upon request." Write it in regular font, without bold or italics, at the bottom of the page, as shown on the sample résumé. Do not include a list of references on your résumé; you can provide that to the prospective employer in a separate document if he or she asks for it.

There are certain guidelines you should follow when choosing your references:

- Make sure a prospective reference is willing to act as a reference for you before you give his or her name to your interviewer. Not only is it polite and professional to do so, it will also allow you to determine whether that individual's referral will be favorable. If the individual hesitates, or seems uncomfortable, you should choose a different reference.
- Prepare an updated copy of your résumé for your reference so that he or she can review your accomplishments and speak more knowledgably about you to the employer.
- If possible, choose as a reference someone who is (or has been) employed in the field in which you are seeking a job.
- It is acceptable to ask a professor to act as a reference. However, choose from among only those professors with whom you have had a class within the past two years; longer than that may indicate to the prospective employer that you are unable to find a more recent referral. In addition, make sure you choose a professor in whose class you did well!

Writing a Cover Letter: An Overview

In addition to writing a well-organized, error-free, and succinct résumé, you must also provide your prospective employer with a succinct and professional cover letter. It is important that you know how to write a well-organized, professional cover letter because it will act as the "gate keeper" for your résumé. If your cover letter is well written, it is more likely that the prospective employer will want to read your résumé. Conversely, if your cover letter is poorly written, it is more likely that your résumé will end up in the "discard" pile.

The Importance of Writing a Good Cover Letter

Students often do not realize the importance of crafting a well-written cover letter. Instead, they treat it as an afterthought, spending little time working on it. The results are often short notes that contain sweeping, generalized statements that lack any significant information.

> **Example of a poorly written cover letter:**
>
> To Whom It May Concern:
>
> I am submitting my résumé for your consideration because I feel that I would be very suitable for the position for which you are hiring due to my experience, knowledge, education, and skills. I am very willing and capable of learning any new skills in order to fulfill the duties required to perform the job.
>
> Thank you for your time, and I look forward to speaking with you.
>
> Sincerely,
>
> Jane Doe

Contrary to what many students think, a cover letter is, in fact, an important part of your application. In essence, a well-written cover letter provides you with your first opportunity to "sell yourself." As such, it should include specific, personal information that strengthens your candidacy for the position. Specifically, you can (and should!) highlight your strengths, skills, and accomplishments while also stating how you can contribute to the organization.

Specific Tips to Follow When Writing a Cover Letter

As with your résumé, the content of your cover letter should be well written, professional, and succinct. When you write a cover letter, there are a few important tips you should follow:

- **Open the letter with a proper greeting by directing it to a specific person.** Begin your letter with "Dear (name)," directing it to the person who is overseeing the application process. If you cannot find that person's name online or in the information you have about the job opening, call the company (or agency) and ask the receptionist for the name of the Human Resources representative. *Do not* use a generic greeting such as, "To Whom It May Concern" or "Dear Sir or Madam."
- **Identify the position you are applying for.** Include the job code or reference number (if one is provided) either in the subject line of your cover letter or in the opening sentence.
- **Do not start your letter by introducing yourself.** Do not begin the narrative of your letter with "My name is ____." This is unprofessional and indicates a lack of experience. Instead, draft an opening sentence that emphasizes your leadership experience, knowledge, or advanced skills that specifically align with the job description. It is important for you to start your letter with a statement that shows the employer your strengths.
- **Do not repeat everything that is included on your résumé.** The purpose of a cover letter is to complement your résumé, not to repeat it. To accomplish this, draft a compelling and concise narrative that emphasizes your most impressive skills that qualify you for the position. You should also include any expertise you have that would strengthen your candidacy for the position. Then, provide a few examples that illustrate why you are the perfect candidate for the job.

- **Keep your letter short.** Your cover letter, like your résumé, should be succinct. Say what you need to say in no more than one page.
- **Conclude your letter with a thank you and a promise to follow up.** Thank the individual for taking the time to read your letter, and promise that you will follow up by telephone or email by a certain date. Write yourself a reminder note to ensure that you follow up by that date.
- **Before sending, proofread your letter carefully.** Cover letters that contain typographical errors, spelling errors, and grammatical mistakes signify to the prospective employer that you lack attention to detail. In addition, they send the message to the prospective employer that your work might also be subpar. Such cover letters and résumés most likely will end up in the "discard" pile. To prevent this from happening, use spell check but do so with caution, because it might miss errors. In addition, proofread multiple drafts before you send your letter. You should also ask someone whom you trust to read your letter to double-check for any errors you may have overlooked.
- **If applying online (or emailing a copy of your cover letter), send it as a .pdf.** Sometimes formatting issues occur when a recipient opens a Word document sent from another person (e.g., extra spacing between words, misaligned margins). Therefore, to avoid these potential problems, always save an extra copy as a .pdf file and send that version electronically.

> **Note!** For further tips and instructions on writing a cover letter, go to the websites www.themuse.com/advice/how-to-write-a-cover-letter-31-tips-you-need-to-know *and* www.monster.com/career-advice/cover-letter-resume/cover-letter-tips

> See **Preparing for the Job Market, Handout #2: "Sample Cover Letter"** at the end of this unit.

> **Note!** If you are writing cover letters for multiple jobs, be sure to customize each cover letter for each particular job.

> See **Preparing for the Job Market, Take-Home Assignment #1: "Writing a Résumé and Cover Letter"** at the end of this unit.

Electronic Communications: An Overview

A significant amount of professional communication occurs electronically. Specifically, many students send an email to inquire about a possible internship opportunity, or to get additional information about a particular job posting. Moreover, many employers require applications to be completed online. Just as it is critical to draft a professional and succinct résumé and cover letter, it is equally important to communicate professionally and succinctly in *all* electronic communications.

Tips for Drafting a Professional Email

There are several tips you should follow to ensure that the emails you send are professional:

- **Send professional emails from a professional email account.** The account from which you send your professional emails should include your name. Do not name your account using nicknames, hobbies, creative phrases, or favorite sports teams. The recipient will take you more seriously if you have a professional email account.

- **State the purpose of your email.** For every email you send, fill in the subject line of the email with a short phrase that summarizes the purpose of your email.
- **Use a proper greeting.** In the salutation, state the name of the person to whom you are sending the email; use his or her formal title and last name (e.g., Captain Smith, Ms. Thompson). Unless you know the recipient personally, do not use his or her first name in your greeting. Use the same salutation in all subsequent correspondences to that person.
- **Be concise.** Keep your emails short. They should not be as brief as a text message, but the recipient should be able to ascertain the purpose of your email within the first two lines. A good email should take no more than 15–30 seconds to read. In addition, if the recipient must scroll down to finish reading your message, edit it so that it all fits onto the first screen.
- **Watch your tone.** Do not write in the same conversational tone you would use if you were sending the email to a friend. Write in complete sentences using proper grammar, spelling, punctuation, and spacing. Do not use slang, abbreviations, or emoticons.
- **End with a strong closing.** Thank the recipient for his or her time, and provide a time frame within which you will send a follow-up email. Also include information about how the recipient can reach you by means other than email. The best way to do this is to set up an automatic signature line in your email account that includes your name, address, email address, telephone number, and links to your personal profile on social media.
- **Proofread carefully.** Carefully proofread and edit your email before you send it. Look for misspellings, homonyms, grammar, and punctuation errors. Careless email mistakes will reflect poorly on you.

Sample Professional Email:

Subject: Directions for Interview
Date: March 19, 2016
From: Jane Doe <jdoe@gmail.com>
To: Director Franklin <mfranklin@osp.va.gov>

Director Franklin,

I will be taking the Metro into the city for my interview next Tuesday. Can you please tell me which line and stop is located closest to the department? When I arrive, is there a specific person I should check in with?

Thank you. I look forward to meeting you next week.

Jane

Jane L. Doe
236 Main Street
Baltimore, MD 21209
(410) 333-5609
jdoe@gmail.com
LinkedIn: www.linkedin.com/in/jane-l-doe-a25018117

Professional Social Media Profiles: An Overview

Before you enter the job market, you should thoroughly evaluate your social media profiles. Many employers will evaluate and screen an applicant's social media profiles before they make a hiring decision.

These profiles include applicants' FaceBook, Instagram, Twitter, and LinkedIn accounts. Employers access these sites to see what type of material the individual has posted, with whom the applicant associates, and the types of behavior in which the applicant and his or her friends engage (Jobvite, 2014).

The Negative Impact of an Unprofessional Social Media Profile

Posting an unprofessional social media profile can have a significant impact on an employer's decision to hire you. In fact, many employers decide not to hire an applicant after they view his or her social media profile. In a study, CareerBuilder (2014) found that over one-half of the employers surveyed reported that they decided *against* hiring a specific applicant because of the negative content they saw on the person's social media sites.

Therefore, before you enter the job market, carefully review your social media profiles for negative content. According to CareerBuilder (2014), there are several common "flags" that negatively affect a job applicant's chances of being hired. These include the following:

- posts of images or information that is sexual or inappropriate,
- posts of images or information relating to drinking or drug use,
- posts of images or information indicating that the individual engaged in criminal activity,
- posts that include discriminatory comments of any nature (e.g., race, sexual orientation),
- posts that include derogatory comments about a previous employer or coworker,
- posts of false and/or exaggerated information about the individual's skills or experience,
- posts that reflect an overall lack of communication skills, and
- use of an inappropriate screen name.

If you are unsure about whether something is, or may be, considered negative, remove it!

Creating a Professional Social Media Profile

In contrast to the potential harm that may be caused by an unprofessional social media profile, creating a professional social media profile can increase your chances of employment. In the same survey conducted by CareerBuilder (2014), one-third of the employers who screened social media profiles stated that the content in an applicant's profile increased the likelihood that they would hire the candidate.

LinkedIn: An Overview

One of the most effective social media platforms to use to search for jobs is LinkedIn (Adams, 2013). Launched in 2003, LinkedIn is a social networking site specifically geared toward the business community (LinkedIn, 2016). Its purpose is to create a platform that enables its users to establish and document professional networks. Thus, this platform allows applicants to search for jobs while also allowing prospective employers to search for qualified candidates. Currently, it has over 400 million members representing over 170 industries, including criminal justice (LinkedIn, 2016).

Many employers and recruiters use LinkedIn. In fact, in a recent survey, over 95% of employers and recruiters reported using LinkedIn to find potential applicants and to vet potential candidates (Adams, 2013; McMullen, 2015). However, individuals seeking jobs are not as likely to use LinkedIn. According to McMullen (2015), fewer than 40% of individuals who were seeking employment reported that they had a LinkedIn profile. With the large numbers of employers and recruiters using LinkedIn to find potential candidates, LinkedIn is an optimal platform for students to use to connect with a potential employer. Thus, you should create a LinkedIn profile as soon as you are ready to enter the job market.

Creating a LinkedIn Profile

Basic membership in LinkedIn is free, and it does not take a lot of time or effort to set up a profile. However, to maximize your exposure and to increase a prospective employer's confidence in you, there are a few tips to follow when you set up your profile:

Professional Social Media Profiles: An Overview

- **Use a professional profile image.** The profile picture is the first image that a prospective employer will see of you, so choose your photograph carefully. Although you do not have to have a professional photographer take your profile picture, your image should project a professional attitude. Use a headshot of yourself; do not have anyone else in the photo with you. Also, dress nicely and smile!
- **Write a strong headline.** Write a concise statement (120 characters or less) that summarizes your best and most valuable professional qualifications.
- **Write a summary that complements your headline.** Include a brief description of who you are and what you want to do. Use keywords that will grab a recruiter's attention.
- **Summarize your employment history.** In this section, if you have been out of high school for more than 10 years, list only the jobs that you have held within the past 10 years. Otherwise, list all of the jobs you have held since high school. Include in this section the name and location of each employer, the position you held, and the length of your employment. Also share some specific accomplishments for each position. This will help highlight the skills and knowledge you gained while you held those positions.
- **List any certifications you have received.** List every certification you have received, even if you do not think it is important.
- **List all of your educational experiences.** Starting with college, list all of the degrees you have earned to date. In addition, specify any disciplines in which you received a "minor" degree (e.g., "majored" in criminal justice, "minored" in ethics). Also, list all of the certificates you have received.
- **Highlight your most valuable skills and expertise.** This is one of the most important elements of your profile because this is often what recruiters and employers will search for when looking for potential applicants. For this section, include at least five key skills and then ask your LinkedIn connections to endorse each skill they know you excel at.
- **Talk about your volunteer experience.** Even though you may not have been paid for your volunteer work, include all of your volunteer experience in your profile. Also include any internships you completed. Listing these experiences is important because they may have helped you develop professional skills that an employer finds valuable.
- **Courses.** Highlight a set of courses you completed that shows recruiters and potential employers the type of knowledge and skills you have learned and developed.
- **Brag about the honors or awards you have earned.** Now is not the time to be humble or shy! Tell potential employers when and how you have been recognized for your achievements.
- **List all of the organizations in which you are a member.** Identify every organization, both professional and academic, in which you are (or were) a member. Highlight any type of leadership role you held within each organization.
- **Do not forget to solicit recommendations.** This is a critical part of your profile. Whom you know is very important! Actively solicit recommendations from professors, current and former employers, and current and former colleagues with whom you worked closely. Also, ask them to share a brief testimonial that addresses any of your skills or expertise. You can never have too many recommendations!
- **Finally, do not forget to update your profile.** Your profile is designed to be a fluid professional portrait. Therefore, update your information on a regular basis. Also, remember to frequently search the LinkedIn database for additional potential connections to add to your network.

See **Preparing for the Job Market, Handout #3: "LinkedIn Profile Checklist"** at the end of this unit.

NOTES

Preparing for the Job Market, Handout #1

Sample Résumé

Jane L. Doe
236 Main Street
Baltimore, MD 21209
(410) 333-5609
jdoe@ubalt.edu

OBJECTIVE
Highly motivated and dependable Bachelor's candidate seeking full-time position in federal law enforcement. More than six years of security and management experience in the private sector, certified as an Emergency Response Coordinator by the American Red Cross, and certified by the International Foundation for Protection Officers.

EDUCATION

Bachelor of Science in Criminology, May 2013
University of Baltimore, Baltimore, MD
Summa Cum Laude

RELATED EXPERIENCE

NORDSTROM—Tysons Corner, VA April 2010–present
Manager of Loss Prevention Operations
- Supervise 25 employees
- Hire and train all new employees
- Facilitate and consult with corporate headquarters in the development and implementation of new security protocols
- Oversee all investigations

NORDSTROM—Tysons Corner, VA March 2009–April 2010
Loss Prevention Specialist
- Prepared theft reports for management
- Assisted manager with employee training and loss prevention
- Created new security protocol for prevention of employee theft

BEST BUY—Towson, MD February 2007–March 2009
Loss Prevention Specialist
- Assisted manager in investigating in-store thefts
- Prepared loss reports

EMPLOYMENT HISTORY

REI—Timonium, MD June 2006–January 2007
Sales Representative
- Assisted customers
- Organized and catalogued inventory
- Assisted manager in training new employees

PIZZA HUT—Towson, MD October 2005–June 2006
Head Hostess
- Supervised waitstaff
- Trained all new front-staff employees
- Assisted manager with payroll

CERTIFICATIONS AND TECHNOLOGICAL SKILLS
- Completed the Certified Protection Officer Program (CPO) through the International Foundation of Protection Officers, June 2010. Recertified: June 2012, June 2014
- Certified as Emergency Response Coordinator through Red Cross of America, June 2009
- Proficient in GIS, SPSS, LexisNexis

ACADEMIC AND PROFESSIONAL HONORS

President's Award—University of Baltimore
- May 2013

Dean's List—University of Baltimore
- Fall 2010 to Spring 2013

COMMUNITY AND PROFESSIONAL ENGAGEMENT

Red Cross of America
- *Volunteer*, 2009 to present

Academy of Criminal Justice Sciences
- *Member*, Fall 2010 to present

International Association of Professional Security Consultants
- *Member,* 2013 to present

Criminal Justice Student Association
University of Baltimore, Baltimore, MD
- *Member*, Fall 2010 to Spring 2013
- *Officer (Secretary)*, Spring 2011 to Spring 2013

References available upon request

Preparing for the Job Market, Handout #2

Sample Cover Letter

Jane Doe
1234 Main Street, Baltimore, MD 21201, 410-555-0123, jdoe@gmail.com

John T. Willow   February 1, 2016
Chief of Police
U.S. Department of Veteran Affairs Police Department
1401 Connecticut Avenue, NW
Washington, DC 20001

Dear Chief Willow,

I am submitting my résumé for consideration for the position of Officer in Training with the U.S. Department of Veteran Affairs Police Department, which was advertised in the Baltimore Sun. I have worked for over nine years in security within the private sector, of which the last six years have been in a supervisory capacity. Within this role I have honed my communication, investigative, and leadership skills.

Currently, I am employed with Nordstrom as the Manager of Loss Prevention Operations at their Tysons Corner store. This is one of the company's busiest retail sites on the East Coast, based on both the volume of customers who visit the store and total retail sales. As the head of the loss prevention operations, I supervise a team of 25 security personnel and am responsible for ensuring the safety of company staff and customers, securing all property, and overseeing all investigations of incidents that involve a security breach. During my nine years in retail security, I have gained a varied skill set that includes the ability to solve problems creatively. For example, when I was a junior security associate at Nordstrom, I developed a new protocol to prevent employee theft; the protocol was subsequently adopted by the corporate office and is now a SOP for all of their retail stores. In my supervisory role, I have similarly developed new protocols to reduce the incidents of retail theft. Consequently, our store has been consistently ranked by the corporate office as one of the top five stores nationally for the fewest security breaches.

I believe I have the required skills to be an effective law enforcement officer in the public sector, and I am eager to learn more about the U.S. Department of Veteran Affairs Police Department. I look forward to an opportunity to speak with you about the position of Officer in Training. Should you have any questions, or would like to schedule an interview, please contact me at 410-555-0123.

Thank you for your time.

Sincerely,

Jane Doe

Enclosure: Résumé

Preparing for the Job Market, Handout #3

LinkedIn Profile Checklist

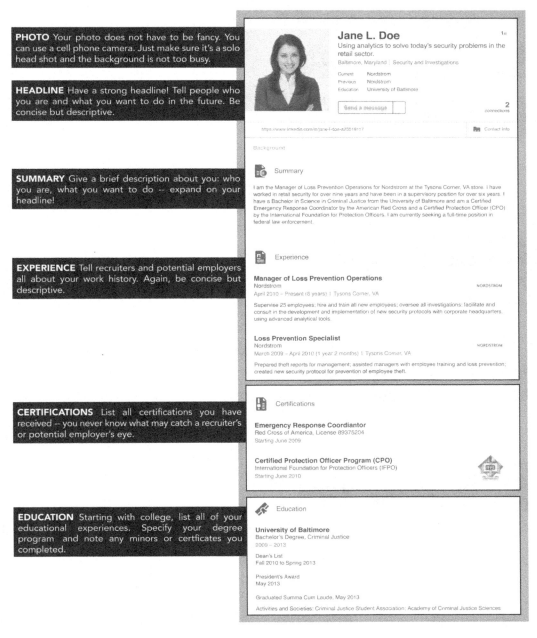

Unit 9 | Preparing for the Job Market

SKILLS & EXPERTISE You should always add at least 5 key skills. Your LinkedIn connections can endorse you for the things you are great at.

VOLUNTEER EXPERIENCE & CAUSES Just because you may not have been paid does not mean it's not important. Recruiters and potential employers often see this as being just as valuable as paid work experience.

COURSES List the classes that show recruiters and potential employers what your skills and interests are.

HONORS & AWARDS Let the world know about any honors or awards you received in school, in the community, or from any professional organization.

ORGANIZATIONS Be sure to list all organizations you have participated in, or are currently participating in.

RECOMMENDATIONS Ask professors, classmates, and employers to write you a recommendation. This will give your skills and strengths extra credibility with recruiters and potential employers.

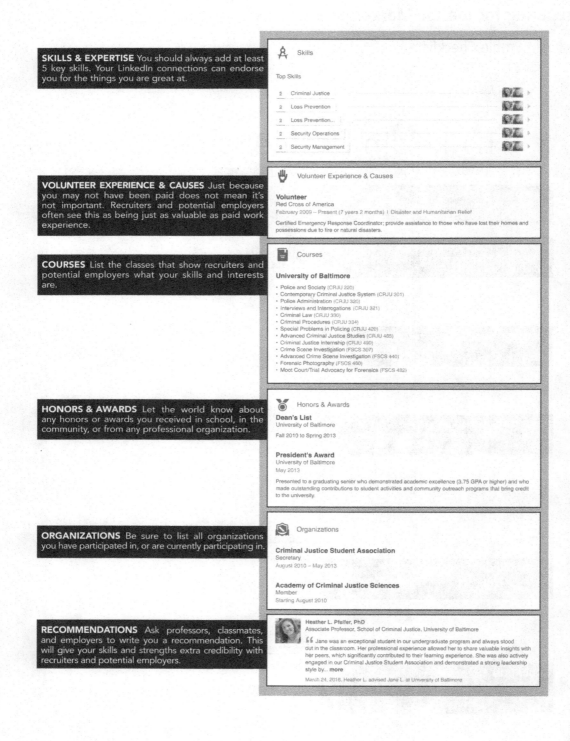

Skills

Top Skills

- 2 Criminal Justice
- 2 Loss Prevention
- 2 Loss Prevention...
- 2 Security Operations
- 2 Security Management

Volunteer Experience & Causes

Volunteer
Red Cross of America
February 2009 – Present (7 years 2 months) | Disaster and Humanitarian Relief

Certified Emergency Response Coordinator; provide assistance to those who have lost their homes and possessions due to fire or natural disasters.

Courses

University of Baltimore

- Police and Society (CRJU 220)
- Contemporary Criminal Justice System (CRJU 301)
- Police Administration (CRJU 320)
- Interviews and Interrogations (CRJU 321)
- Criminal Law (CRJU 330)
- Criminal Procedures (CRJU 334)
- Special Problems in Policing (CRJU 420)
- Advanced Criminal Justice Studies (CRJU 485)
- Criminal Justice Internship (CRJU 490)
- Crime Scene Investigation (FSCS 307)
- Advanced Crime Scene Investigation (FSCS 440)
- Forensic Photography (FSCS 460)
- Moot Court/Trial Advocacy for Forensics (FSCS 482)

Honors & Awards

Dean's List
University of Baltimore
Fall 2010 to Spring 2013

President's Award
University of Baltimore
May 2013

Presented to a graduating senior who demonstrated academic excellence (3.75 GPA or higher) and who made outstanding contributions to student activities and community outreach programs that bring credit to the university.

Organizations

Criminal Justice Student Association
Secretary
August 2010 – May 2013

Academy of Criminal Justice Sciences
Member
Starting August 2010

Heather L. Pfeifer, PhD
Associate Professor, School of Criminal Justice, University of Baltimore

" Jane was an exceptional student in our undergraduate program and always stood out in the classroom. Her professional experience allowed her to share valuable insights with her peers, which significantly contributed to their learning experience. She was also actively engaged in our Criminal Justice Student Association and demonstrated a strong leadership style by... more

March 24, 2016, Heather L. advised Jane L. at University of Baltimore

Preparing for the Job Market, Take-Home Assignment #1

Writing a Résumé and Cover Letter

Write a chronological résumé and a cover letter following the format taught in class. The résumé and the cover letter must be printed on résumé-quality paper. The résumé should be no more than two pages long.

Preparing Professional Reports and Presentations

UNIT 10

UNIT SUMMARY
Learning Objectives
Writing in a Professional Setting: An Overview
Writing in the Criminal Justice Profession
    Police Reports: An Overview
        Writing an Incident Report
    Risk Assessment Instruments: An Overview
        Types of Risk Assessment Instruments
        Completing a Risk/Needs Assessment Instrument
    Child Protective Services Intake Form: An Overview
        Completing a Child Protective Services Intake Form
Preparing a Professional PowerPoint Presentation: An Overview
    Guidelines for Creating and Delivering a PowerPoint Presentation
        Organizing a PowerPoint Presentation
        Creating a Visually Engaging PowerPoint Presentation
            Selecting a Font for a PowerPoint Presentation
            Selecting Colors for a PowerPoint Presentation
            How to Add a Chart or a Graph to a PowerPoint Presentation
            How to Add a Photograph (or an Image) to a PowerPoint Presentation
        Delivering a PowerPoint Presentation

Learning Objectives

At the end of this unit, students will be able to do the following:
- Complete an Incident Report for law enforcement.
- Complete a Risk/Needs Assessment Instrument for probation and parole.
- Complete a Child Protective Services Intake Form.
- Create and deliver a well-organized and visually engaging PowerPoint presentation.

Writing in a Professional Setting: An Overview

Writing is an integral part of every profession. According to a report released by The National Commission on Writing, more than half of the companies surveyed stated that "they 'frequently' or 'almost always' produce technical reports (59 percent), formal reports (62 percent), and memos and correspondence (70 percent)" (College Board, 2004, p. 4). As such, employers consider an individual's professional writing abilities to be a "threshold skill" when they decide whether to hire or promote that individual (College Board, 2004). Moreover, in a national survey of over 120 major employers, supervisors reported they were unlikely to hire an individual who could not write or communicate clearly, because a significant portion of today's job duties involve some form of writing (College Board, 2004). Therefore, it is important that you know how to write well in a professional setting.

Writing in the Criminal Justice Profession

As with the majority of professions, writing is an integral part of the criminal justice profession; *every* criminal justice agency requires that you write. Thus, regardless of whether you pursue a career in law enforcement, juvenile justice, or probation and parole, you will spend a significant amount of your time writing.

Typically, criminal justice professionals are required to write a variety of professional reports. Although different reports serve different purposes, they all must be well written because their information might be used to make critical decisions. These decisions could include those that affect an individual's life and liberty, as well as how resources should be allocated within departments and agencies. Because these reports play a significant role in the day-to-day operations of the criminal justice system, in many criminal justice agencies, your writing skills can positively or negatively affect your chances for promotion (Hoots, 2014).

Three types of agencies that require that you write reports are law enforcement, probation and parole, and child protective services. Because many criminal justice students pursue careers in these fields, we will discuss how to properly prepare an entry-level report for each agency: an Incident Report (law enforcement), a Risk/Needs Assessment Instrument (probation and parole), and a Child Protective Services Intake Form (child protective services).

Incident Reports: An Overview

One type of report that police officers are required to complete is an Incident Report. This type of report is completed by police officers who have been deployed to a scene. In the report, they provide a detailed and factual account of the alleged incident, along with identifying information about any witnesses and victims. A supervising officer reviews the information contained in the report to determine whether the incident meets the elements of a criminal offense. If it does, the case is forwarded to a detective for further investigation. If it does not, the case is closed.

Significantly, most police officers spend more of their time completing such reports than any other job-related task and, as such, they must be well written, well organized, and thorough (Hoots, 2014). According to Hoots, it is important that the Incident Report be well written for three reasons. First, it is the "starting point" of any investigation; without a formal report, there is nothing to investigate. Therefore, the report must be thorough and well written so that the supervising officer can make an informed and correct decision about the future of the case. Second, a well-written report allows the officer (and the department) to spend less time solving or clearing a case. Conversely, when a report is poorly written, a prosecutor is more likely to challenge an officer's credibility, potentially resulting in a failed prosecution of an offender. Finally, the report must be well written because the quality of the officer's report may affect his or her professional reputation, as well as play a role in whether he or she receives promotions (Hoots, 2014).

In addition to being well written, it is vitally important that Incident Reports contain accurate and detailed information. This includes information about the actions of the officers, victims, and suspects, as well as all observations made by the officers. It is important that the officers accurately record this information because the supervising officer will use it to determine whether further investigation is warranted. If an officer fails to accurately include *all* of the detailed and important information in his or her report, an investigating officer may erroneously conclude that further investigation is not warranted. Similarly, he or she may conclude that it is warranted when, in fact, a more detailed and accurate report would have shown otherwise.

In this section you will learn how to write a thorough, well-written, and concise Incident Report.

Writing an Incident Report

At the police academy, new recruits are taught that an Incident Report should include the answers to as many of the following questions as possible: Who?, What?, Where?, When?, Why?, and How? However, when officers prepare their reports, they should not just answer each of those questions. Instead, they should carefully record the chronology of the events of the incident and write the report in a clear and concise manner.

When you write an Incident Report, there are several rules you should follow:

- When you fill in the identifying information on the form, be sure to spell correctly the name of each involved individual and to accurately record each address, telephone number, race, gender, and date of birth.
- When you fill in the information about the description of the suspect(s), be sure it is complete and thorough. Information you should list includes approximate height and weight, hair color and length, eye color, and any distinguishing features such as facial hair, tattoos, scars, piercings, or birthmarks.
- If items were taken in the incident, be sure to accurately record the description of each item, including its age (new or used), serial number if available, and approximate value.
- Your narrative should be specific and detailed. However, this does *not* mean it should be lengthy; rather, you should include all of the important information in a concise but clear manner. In addition,
    - Write your narrative using full sentences and proper grammar. Use formal language; do not use slang (e.g., write "disturbance," rather than "ruckus").
    - Do not embellish the facts or add to them to make your narrative "flow." Adding incorrect or irrelevant information can have adverse consequences; it can affect your supervisor's decision about whether to pursue a case, and could affect your credibility if you are required to testify about the incident.
    - Write your narrative objectively. State the facts without injecting your personal opinions.

- When you write your narrative, be precise regarding *who* was involved, *what* happened, *when* the incident occurred, *where* the incident occurred, *why* the incident occurred, and *how* the incident occurred.
- In your narrative, you should also include each of the following:
  - A description of the crime;
  - What steps the officer(s) took in the investigative process;
  - A statement from each victim;
  - A statement from each witness;
  - Information pertaining to the collection of the evidence (e.g., what evidence was collected, where it was located at the scene, how it was catalogued/recorded); and
  - A description of any property damage.
- At the end of the narrative, include any information you have about potential suspects. This includes a complete description of each individual, with each address, telephone number, date of birth, and social security number. In addition, include any other information you have that indicates why each individual is, or may be, considered to be a suspect.
- At the end of the report, include your name as the reporting officer, your ID and division number, and the name of your precinct (or district). Also include that same information for the detective assigned to the case.
- *Importantly*, proofread your narrative carefully. When you proofread it, make sure the content is accurate, the narrative is cohesive (e.g., well organized), and there are no mechanical or grammatical errors.

See the following handouts at the end of this unit:

Preparing Professional Reports and Presentations, Handout #1: "Crime Scene Report: A Case Study"

Preparing Professional Reports and Presentations, Handout #2: "Incident Report"

Preparing Professional Reports and Presentations, Take-Home Assignment #1: "Preparing an Incident Report"

Note! An electronic copy of the Incident Report is available that will allow you to enter the information directly onto the form. If you do not have an e-book, ask your instructor for a copy of the .pdf file or fill out the Incident Report form located at the end of this unit.

Risk Assessment Instruments: An Overview

Another type of instrument that criminal justice professionals may be required to fill out is a Risk Assessment Instrument. The practice of risk assessment focuses on the likelihood that an individual will engage in a variety of negative behaviors (James, 2015). Social scientists believe that by identifying patterns of behaviors within groups of individuals, they can estimate the potential risk of whether an individual who shares characteristics with the group will engage in similar behavior (James, 2015).

Traditionally, the most common predicted outcome of risk assessment for offenders is recidivism. However, it has also been used for other purposes, such as estimating the likelihood that an individual will fail to appear for assigned court dates, escape from custody, pose a security risk within the institution, or violate conditions of supervision in the community (James, 2015). Given the prevalence of these instruments in the criminal justice system, in this section, we will discuss the different types of instruments that are used and how to fill them out.

Types of Risk Assessment Instruments

Currently, there are two types of actuarial risk instruments used by criminal justice agencies (James, 2015). The first type involves static risk scales that rely exclusively on risk factors that do not change over time (e.g., demographics) or that are unidirectional (e.g., criminal history). The second type, a risk/needs assessment, includes a broader range of correlates of crime. These instruments include criminal history variables, as well as a select number of social and contextual variables that are shown to contribute or diminish an individual's likelihood of reoffending. Often referred to within the literature as "criminogenic needs," these factors typically focus on areas of the offender's life that are amenable to change, such as family functioning, deviant associations, and drug use (James, 2015).

Researchers and practitioners argue that by modifying or diminishing risk factors through specific individualized treatment plans, agencies can help reduce an offender's probability of recidivism (Bonta, 2002). Moreover, unlike those instruments that focus exclusively on an offender's criminal history, Risk/Needs Instruments enable an agency to monitor *change* in an offender's behavior (Bonta, 2002). Through regular reassessment, agencies can make adjustments to security classifications or programming that will best reflect an offender's current level of risk (Bonta, 2002).

Currently, many different Risk/Needs Instruments are used by various criminal justice agencies (James, 2015). The structure of these instruments varies greatly. Some risk/needs assessments include a large number of items, whereas others include only a few items. The scoring protocol used for each instrument also varies (James, 2015). Some use a binomial scoring system that requires each item to be scored either a 0 or a 1, based on its absence or presence, and others use a weighted scoring system that allows the individual to assign a continuous score (e.g., 0, 1, 2, 3) for each item.

In this unit, we will discuss how to complete a risk/needs assessment using a small number of items and a weighted scoring system. We have chosen to use this structure because many agencies are increasingly relying on criminogenic risk factors, and they use this type of scoring system. They then use the results to help them make decisions about the appropriate level of supervision and proper case management.

Completing a Risk/Needs Assessment Instrument

See the following handouts at the end of this unit:

Preparing Professional Reports and Presentations, Handout #1: "Crime Scene Report: A Case Study"

Preparing Professional Reports and Presentations, Handout #3: "Preparing a Risk Assessment System–Community Supervision Screening Tool (RAS-CSST)

Preparing Professional Reports and Presentations, Take-Home Assignment #2: "Preparing a Risk Assessment System–Community Supervision Screening Tool (RAS-CSST)"

Note! An electronic copy of the RAS-CSST is available that will allow you to enter the information directly onto the form. If you do not have an e-book, ask your instructor for a copy of the .pdf file or fill out the RAS-CSST form located at the end of this unit.

There are several rules you should follow when you complete a Risk/Needs Assessment instrument:

- In the first section, fill in the subject's name, the assessment date, an APR number (case number), and the name of the assigned probation officer.
- In the next section, use a weighted scoring system (e.g., 0, 1, 2, 3) to score each item on the instrument. Use the information provided in the Incident Report to answer each item.
- Add the scores and record a total.
- Using the total score, classify the individual's risk for reoffending (e.g., low, medium, high).
- Using this classification, write a recommendation for the individual, including a description of an appropriate level of supervision and services that should be incorporated into the case plan to address his or her criminogenic needs. *Criminogenic needs* are those factors in the offender's life that are amenable to change, such as family functioning, deviant associations, and drug use.

Child Protective Services Intake Form: An Overview

Another type of report you may be required to write as a criminal justice professional is a Child Protective Services Intake Form. This type of report is prepared by a staff member of Child Protective Services (CPS) in response to a report about a child's welfare. CPS is responsible for protecting children from harm and for providing support to families in order to help reduce the risk of harm to children (Child Welfare Information Gateway, n.d.). To accomplish this, CPS staff members investigate all forms of child maltreatment, including physical abuse, sexual abuse, mental (emotional) abuse, and neglect. CPS staff members may also complete assessments of a child's and family's needs in order to identify possible interventions and services that can help support the family's efforts to provide a safe and nurturing environment (Child Welfare Information Gateway, n.d.). In addition, CPS professionals often work with law enforcement, courts, and other community agencies that are similarly charged with assisting at-risk children and their families. If you work for CPS, it is very likely that you will be asked to write a CPS Intake Report. Therefore, we will discuss how to do that in this section.

Completing a Child Protective Services Intake Form

When CPS staff receive a report from a "mandatory reporter" (e.g., a teacher, physician, counselor, therapist, child care provider) or from a private citizen alerting them to concerns about a child's welfare, they may initiate an investigation to determine if the child has been, or is, at risk of being harmed (Child Welfare Information Gateway, n.d.). One of the CPS caseworkers will then record that information in a CPS Intake Form.

There are several rules you should follow when you fill out a CPS Intake Form:

- When you fill in the identifying information, be sure to correctly spell the name and accurately record the age or date of birth, address, telephone number, place of employment, and name of school or child care center of each involved individual.
- Answer *every* question on the form. Inadvertently excluding *any* information may affect the case. If you do not have an answer for a question, write "unknown," "suspected," or another answer that indicates that you have read and answered the question to the best of your knowledge.
- Include as much information as possible for each question. Where applicable, address the *who, what, where, why, when,* and *how* as they relate to the situation.
- Answer each question with full sentences following proper grammar and the mechanics of writing rules (see Unit 5 for review). However, if your answer is "unknown," "suspected," or a similar type of answer, it is acceptable to just write the one word.

- Proofread your report carefully: Make sure the content is accurate and there are no mechanical or grammatical errors. Also review it for spacing and spelling errors.

Note! An electronic copy of the CPS Intake Form is available that will allow you to enter the information directly onto the form. If you do not have an e-book, ask your instructor for a copy of the .pdf file or fill out the CPS Intake Form located at the end of this unit.

See the following handouts at the end of this unit:
Preparing Professional Reports and Presentations, Handout #4: "Child Protective Services: A Case Study"
Preparing Professional Reports and Presentations, Handout #5: "Preparing a Child Protective Services Intake Form"
Preparing Professional Reports and Presentations, Take-Home Assignment #3: "Preparing a Child Protective Services Intake Form"

Preparing a Professional PowerPoint Presentation: An Overview

Writing skills are not the only criteria employers use to evaluate their employees' communication skills. According to a national survey of over 120 major American companies, employers similarly expect the individuals they hire to have strong oral communication skills (College Board, 2004). In fact, many jobs will require you to prepare and deliver a formal presentation to either an internal audience (e.g., team, department) or an external audience (e.g., conference, stakeholder meeting). One platform that professionals predominantly rely on for such presentations is PowerPoint. Thus, it is important that you know how to create a visually engaging and cohesive PowerPoint presentation and that you deliver it in a professional manner.

Guidelines for Creating and Delivering a PowerPoint Presentation

Note! The information presented in this section is summarized from a handout provided by the Langsdale Library at the University of Baltimore. To obtain a copy of the handout, go to the website ubalt.libguides.com/powerpoint.

There are three important rules you should follow when you create and deliver an effective PowerPoint presentation:

1. It must be well organized.
2. It must be visually engaging.
3. You must deliver it in a professional manner and within the allotted time frame..

Organizing a PowerPoint Presentation

The first step in preparing your presentation is to map out what you want to say. This is similar to writing an outline for a paper. First, write down the main points you want to cover in your presentation. Then, for each of the main points, write two or three supporting facts (or ideas) that you feel are important to include.

After you have written the main ideas with their supporting points, use that information to create your PowerPoint slides. Specifically, create a new slide for each of your main points. On each slide, include a *few* supporting facts and ideas. Do not overload your slide with a lot of content! Because you will have a limited amount of space for information on the slide, you will need to be selective about what you add.

 Remember that when you do a PowerPoint presentation, *you* are the main focus of the presentation, not the PowerPoint slides! Thus, you will convey the majority of the information in your oral presentation; you will use the slides only to reinforce and support what you say.

Creating a Visually Engaging PowerPoint Presentation

The second step in preparing your presentation is to make your PowerPoint presentation visually engaging. This means it must be easy to read and visually dynamic. To make your PowerPoint presentation easy to read, you will need to select the proper font size and style.

Choosing a Font for a PowerPoint Presentation

When you choose a font size, choose one that is large enough to allow the people sitting in the back of the room to easily read it. In addition, select a simple font style. Do not choose a fancy, decorative style in an attempt to make your slides creative. Remember, this is a professional presentation!

There are several good font styles to use. These include: Baskerville, Bodoni, Franklin Gothic, Garamond, Gill Sans, Helvetica, and Rockwell. It is acceptable to change the size of the font or its weight (e.g., bold, italics) in your slides, but do not mix font styles. Choose one and stick with it! When you choose your font style, pick a style that you think best fits the subject of your presentation and your audience.

Choosing Colors for a PowerPoint Presentation

You should also make your PowerPoint presentation visually dynamic. To do this, incorporate some colors, and add some images or graphics. When you choose your colors, do so carefully because color choice is critical. Too much color can distract the audience, but, too little color can be boring.

When you choose your colors, use either a monochromatic color scheme that uses varying shades of one hue, or an analogous color scheme that uses two hues that are next to each other on the color wheel (e.g., blue and green, or red and orange). You should also carefully select the background color of your slides; a lighter background is better if you are going to present them with the lights on, however, a darker background is better if you are going to present them with the lights off.

How to Add a Chart or a Graph to a PowerPoint Presentation

After you have chosen your colors, the next step is to incorporate some images or graphics into your slides. Graphics will break up the monotony of the text and will help keep your audience engaged. You do not need to include a visual element on every slide, but you should include enough visuals to avoid having too many text-only slides in a row. Visual elements may include a graph (e.g. table, bar chart, pie chart) or a photograph.

If your presentation includes potentially complex material, charts and graphs are a good tool to use to present that material. For example, if you have a significant amount of statistical data, you should present the information in the form of a chart or graph rather than simply listing the numbers. Doing this will make your presentation more interesting and allow your audience to more easily follow what you are saying.

Because many criminal justice presentations will require the inclusion of statistical data, we will discuss how to add charts to your PowerPoint presentation.

Preparing a Professional PowerPoint Presentation: An Overview   253

Note! Because Microsoft Office for Mac uses a different operating platform than Microsoft Office for a PC does, the graphics on your PowerPoint slides may vary slightly from those that are presented in this section. However, the content and the steps are the same for both operating systems.

To add a chart to your PowerPoint presentation, follow this step-by-step visual guide:

Step 1: To add a chart, click on the **Insert Chart** icon shown in the following screenshot.

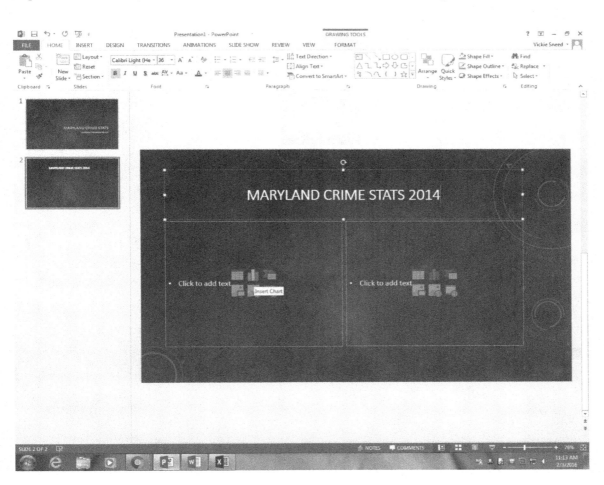

Step 2: A pop-up screen will appear, giving you options for different styles of charts. Click on the type of chart that best suits your needs (e.g., **Column**, **Line**, **Bar**, **Pie**).

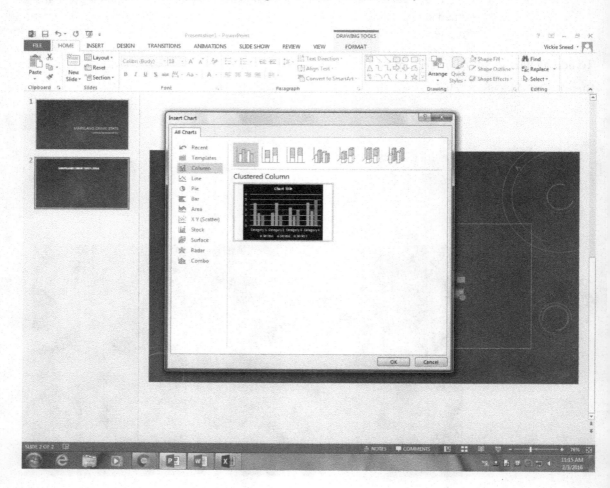

Preparing a Professional PowerPoint Presentation: An Overview

Step 3: Once you have selected a chart style, a prepopulated chart will appear on your slide. Below it, you will see a mini-Excel spreadsheet. This spreadsheet will help you create your chart using the information (e.g., data) that you input.

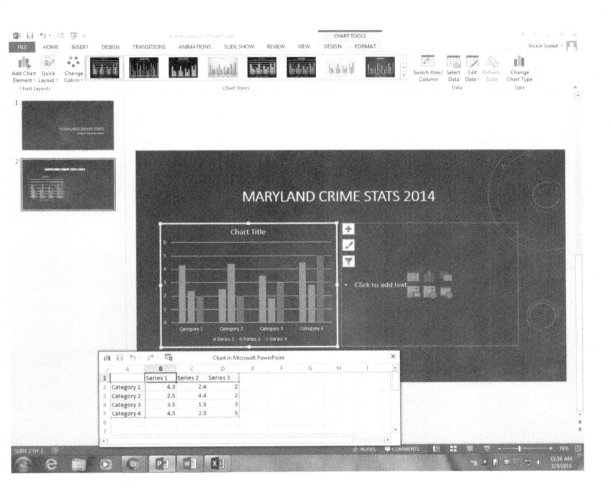

256 Unit 10 | Preparing Professional Reports and Presentations

Step 4: In Row 1, under each column (starting with Column B), add your "Series" names. You can add as many series names as you need. For the purpose of this example, we will use two: "Violent Crimes" and "Property Crimes." In this particular chart, each of these titles then shows up as a specific color in the bar graph.

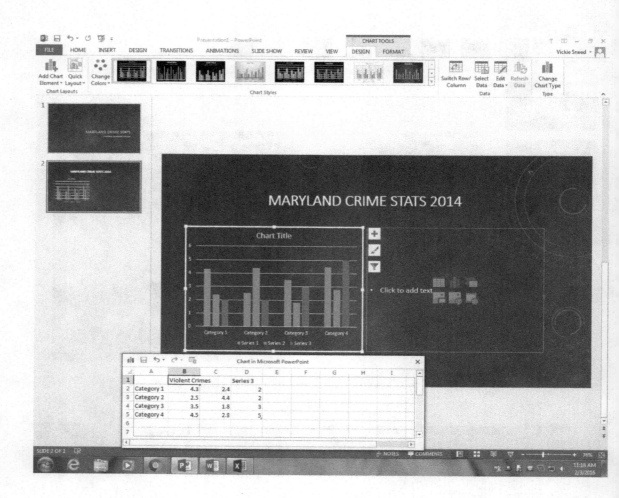

Preparing a Professional PowerPoint Presentation: An Overview   257

Step 5: Because only two series are being used in this example, you must delete Series 3 (e.g., Column D). To do this, highlight the entire column, right click your mouse, and then click on the **Delete** option from the pop-up menu.

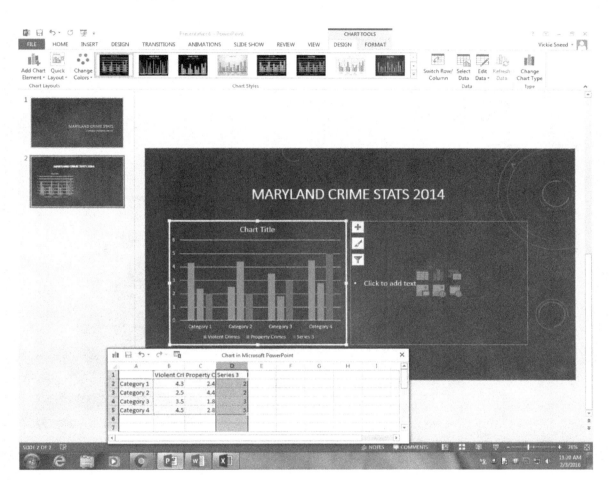

Step 6: Add your categories, which are listed on each row under Column A. You can fill as many rows as you need. For example, in this chart, each row lists a year (e.g., 2013, 2014). Then, for each row, tab over and enter the specific data under each of your column headings (e.g., Violent Crimes, Property Crimes). As you can see when you compare this slide with the slide in the previous screenshot, the chart is being populated into the slide as the data are entered.

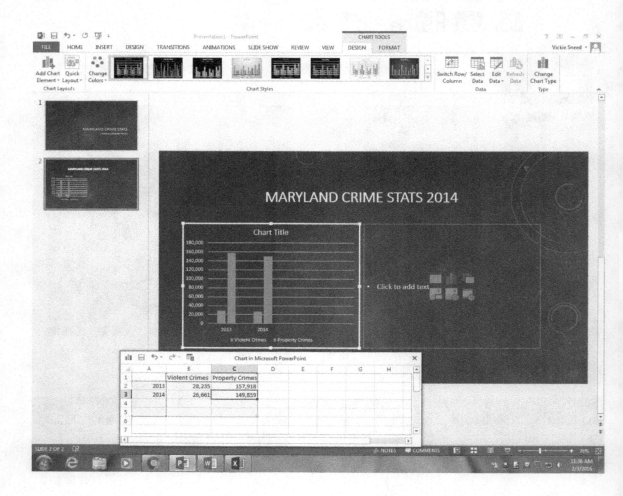

Preparing a Professional PowerPoint Presentation: An Overview

Step 7: Add a title to your chart. To do this, move your cursor over the default setting **Chart Title** and click on it to highlight it. Type in the new name.

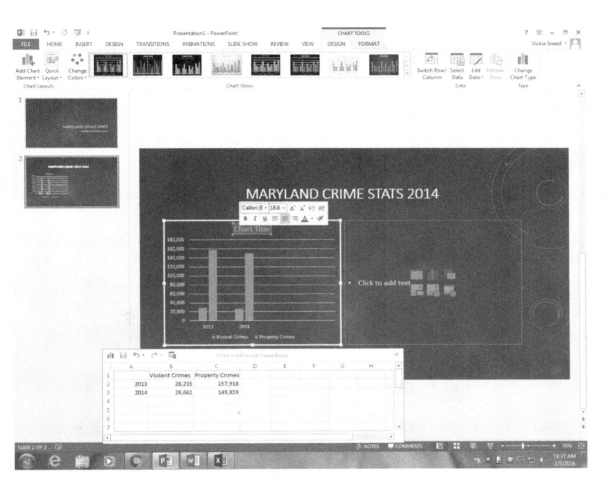

Step 8: When you present statistical data in any bar graph or line graph, always add an axis title along the *y*-axis (vertical axis) to identify the unit of measurement for the data presented (e.g., Number of Arrests, Rates per 100,000). To add an axis title, click on **FILE** and scroll down to **Axis Titles**. Another pop-up screen will appear that will then allow you to select either a horizontal axis or a vertical axis. Click on the option you wish to create.

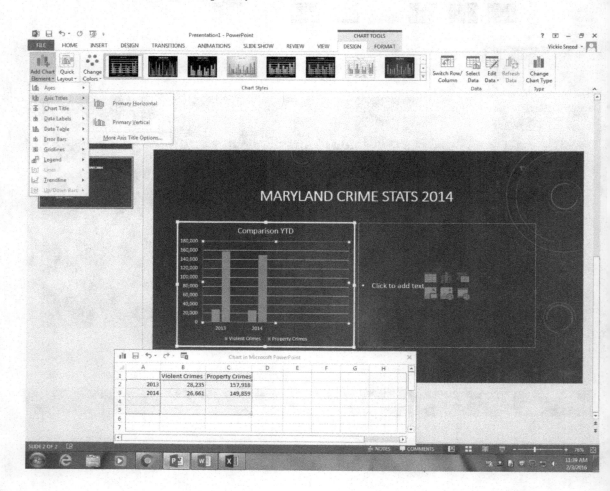

Preparing a Professional PowerPoint Presentation: An Overview   261

Step 9: Change the axis title so it correctly identifies the type of data you are presenting (e.g., Number of Arrests, Rates per 100,000). To change the title, click on the default **Axis Title** until the entire label is highlighted, and then type the new name.

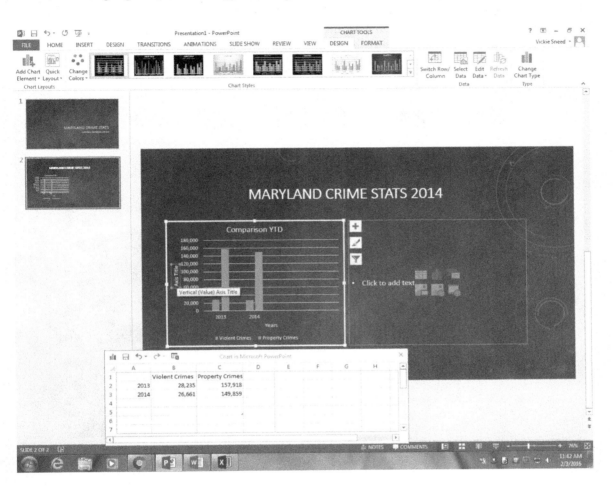

Step 10: You can change the style of your chart after you have created it. To change the style, move your cursor over the chart and click on it. The **CHART TOOLS** tab will appear at the top of your screen. Run your cursor along each tab. As you do this, the chart you created in the slide will change, giving you a preview of each different style. When you find a chart you like, click on it. The chart you had in your slide will automatically change to that new style.

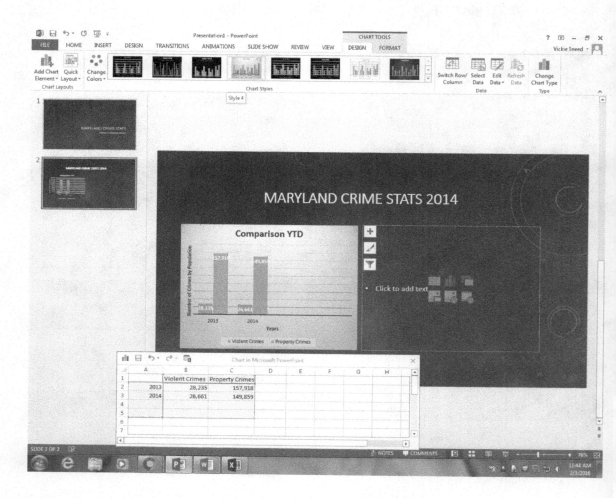

How to Add a Photograph (or an Image) to a PowerPoint Presentation

Another way to make your presentation more interesting and more engaging is to incorporate a few photographs. In general, when you select an image, you should select photographs that look professional (e.g., uncluttered, clear).

 The first thing you must do before you use a photograph in your presentation is to make sure you have permission to do so! Most photographs you find online are copyright protected. This means you cannot use these images without permission.

Although you cannot use a photograph that is copyright protected, there are many stock photograph companies (e.g., Shutterstock, Corbis, Stocksy, Getty) that will allow you to license an image for a small fee. In addition, there are a few sites that allow you to use images for free. These include Creative Commons (search.creativecommons.org) and Flickr (www.flickr.com/search/advanced/).

Preparing a Professional PowerPoint Presentation: An Overview   263

Note! When you search Flickr's database, you will need to scroll to the bottom of the page and select the option that will restrict the results to only those items with a Creative Commons license. A Creative Commons license is a public copyright license that enables anyone to use the material for free.

Note! Because Microsoft Office for Mac uses a different operating platform from that of Microsoft Office for a PC, the graphics on your PowerPoint slides may vary slightly from those that are presented in this section. However, the content and the steps are the same for both operating systems.

To add a photograph or image to your PowerPoint presentation, follow this step-by-step visual guide:

Step 1: Choose the slide layout that best suits your needs. You can view different layouts by clicking on **Layout**, which is located at the left-hand side of the toolbar at the top of your screen (next to **New Slide**).

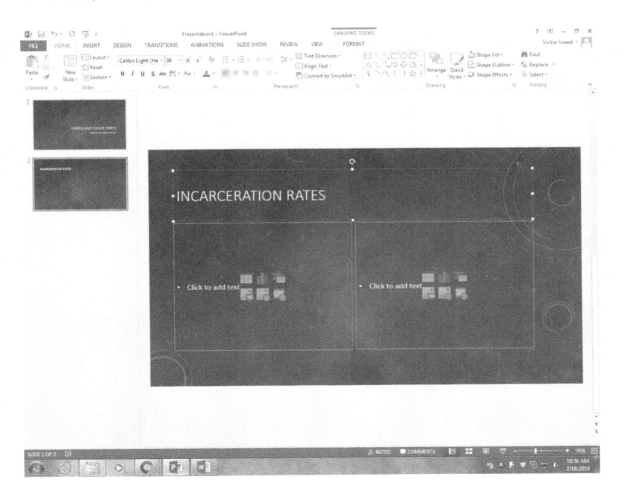

Step 2: Six icons will appear in the center of the slide. Scroll your mouse over each icon until you find the **Pictures** icon. Click on it.

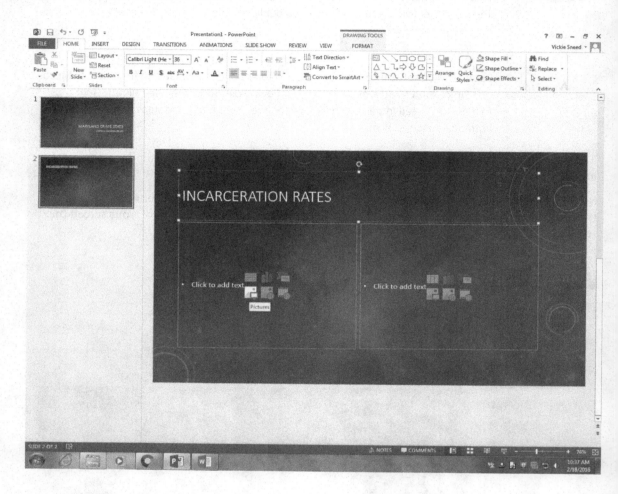

Preparing a Professional PowerPoint Presentation: An Overview   265

Step 3: The **Insert Picture** pop-up screen will appear. Choose the file where the photograph you wish to use is stored.

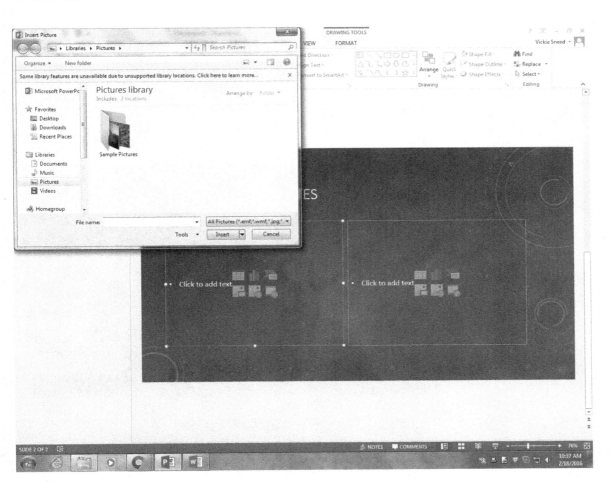

Unit 10 | Preparing Professional Reports and Presentations

Step 4: When you find your photograph, click on it to highlight it, and then click on the **Insert** button at the bottom-right corner of the pop-up screen (next to **Tools**).

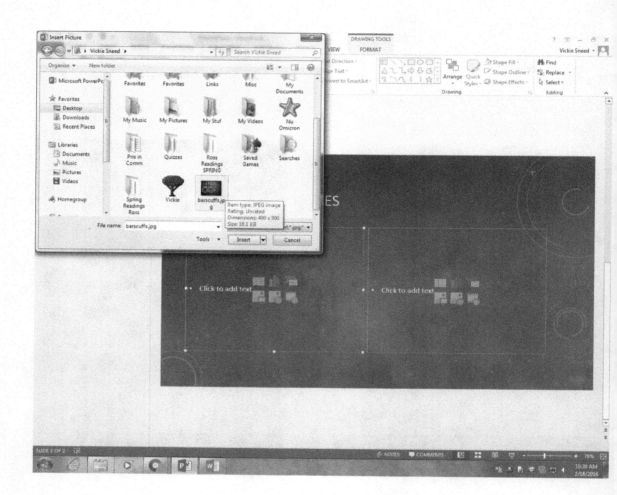

Preparing a Professional PowerPoint Presentation: An Overview

Step 5: Your photograph will now appear, replacing the icons. To add text in the adjoining box, click on **Click to add text**.

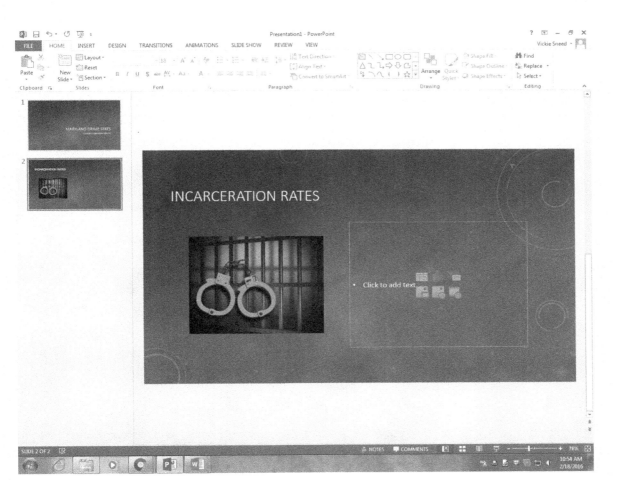

Step 6: A miniature font toolbar will appear. This will allow you to select the font style, text size, and text position (e.g., left, center, right).

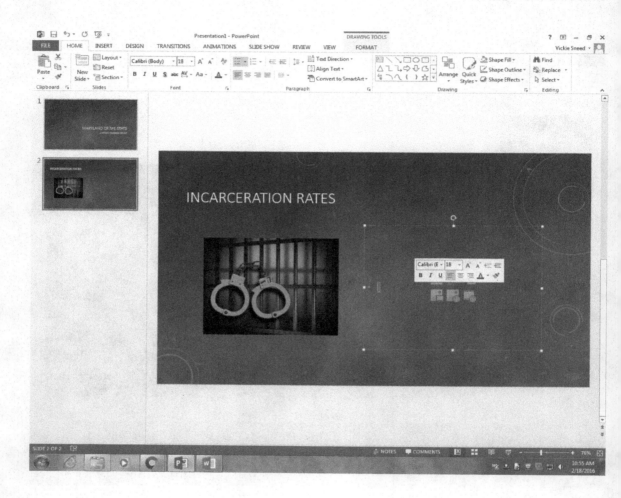

Step 7: Type the text. Keep in mind that in most slides, bullet points are already prepopulated, so if you hit **RETURN** to begin another sentence, it will show up as another bulleted point. If you need to edit the font style, size, or position of your text, simply highlight the text and select the appropriate options from the toolbar located at the top of your screen.

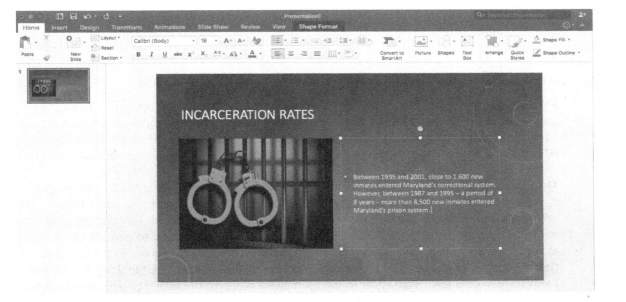

Delivering Your PowerPoint Presentation

The third rule you need to follow when you create a PowerPoint presentation is that you must be able to deliver it within the time frame you are allotted and in an interesting and engaging manner. To ensure that you are able to present it within your time frame, you should practice your presentation several times to determine its length. It is important that you practice it more than once because the more you practice it, the more proficient at it you will become. If you discover that you consistently run over your allotted time, go through your content and delete anything that is extraneous or unimportant.

In addition to being sensitive to time constraints, you should also focus on ways to keep your audience interested and engaged during your presentation. To do this, follow these tips:

- **Do *not* read your slides.** This is perhaps *the* most important rule when you give a PowerPoint presentation. Remember, *you* are the focus of the presentation; your slides are secondary. Moreover, your audience can (and will!) read your slides themselves. Thus, your role is to educate your audience about your topic while using the slides solely as a framework for your discussion.
- **Do *not* read your notes.** It is important that you keep your audience interested and engaged; if you read your notes, you will lose their attention. In order to present your information without your notes, you should practice your presentation until you are very comfortable with it. The more comfortable you feel, the more likely you will be able to periodically look at the audience. Ideally, you should make eye contact with different people in the audience throughout your presentation. However, if you are uncomfortable about making eye contact, focus instead on a few visual spots in the room. This will give the audience the impression that you are looking at and engaging with them.
- **Modulate your tone.** One of the fastest ways to lose an audience's interest is to speak in a monotone. Therefore, when you speak, try to use the same tone of voice you use when you have a conversation with a friend. A lively, personable tone will make your presentation more interesting, and it will help keep your audience's attention.
- **Try to move away from the podium.** A podium serves as barrier between you and the audience and interferes with your ability to connect with them. Therefore, you should stand in front of the podium rather than behind it. If you feel confident, you can walk around the front of the room while you speak. This gives the impression that you are relaxed and comfortable, making it more likely that the audience will connect with you.

NOTES

Preparing Professional Reports and Presentations, Handout #1

Crime Scene Report: A Case Study

Crime Scene Scenario

You are an officer for the Lovettsville Police Department. You and your partner, Officer Susan Blacksmith, have been working burglary detail for the past two weeks. Your work assignment includes patrolling North Avenue, an area comprising primarily commercial businesses and restaurants. Recently, there has been an increase in the number of property crimes in the area, including larceny-thefts and burglaries. Most of those burglaries have involved commercial establishments that sell items that are easy for an offender to "fence" or sell to local pawnshops. On Wednesday, July 15, 2016, at approximately 9:30 p.m., you and Officer Blacksmith are dispatched to investigate a silent alarm report at Peterson's Jewelers at 3534 North Avenue, Lovettsville, Michigan. The telephone number is 401-332-7823.

Law Enforcement Intelligence Background Information

Recent police reports show that there has been a marked increase in the number of burglaries at commercial establishments on North Avenue. According to the reports, the two categories of items most often stolen are jewelry and electronic equipment (e.g., cameras, cell phones). The reports list two primary suspects in several of the burglaries: Thomas "Tiny" Kennedy and Tiffany Briggs. According to police records, Kennedy's date of birth is March 9, 1988, and his Social Security number is 443-33-8239. He is Caucasian, 5'6" tall and weighs approximately 140 pounds. He has a chipped front tooth and a pierced right eyebrow. Kennedy was arrested four times previously for possession of a controlled substance, and twice for possession with intent to distribute. Kennedy's last known address is 633 Baker Street, which is two blocks south of North Avenue. His last know telephone number is 401-932-8474.

Police records also reveal that Kennedy associates with Tiffany Briggs, who had several burglary arrests as a juvenile, and three drug arrests as an adult. Briggs' date of birth is September 1, 1989, and her Social Security number is 204-87-7687. She is African American, 5'4" tall, and weighs approximately 110 pounds. She has a large scar running across her left hand. Briggs' last known address is 8214 Tolliver Avenue, which is next door to Northgate Pawn, a store that has been cited by police several times for fencing stolen merchandise. Her last known telephone number is 401-366-9249.

Crime Scene Investigation

You and Officer Blacksmith arrive at the scene at 9:40 p.m. You immediately observe that a metal recycling container has been pushed up against the east side of the building beneath a window that is approximately 5 feet off the ground. You check the front of the store and find that it is secure, and then you move to the east side of the store. You discover that the window is broken and observe glass on the ground next to the container. When you shine your flashlight on the ground, you observe three footprints that appear to have been made by athletic or tennis shoes. One of the shoe prints is consistent with a men's size 11–12 shoe; the other two shoe prints are consistent with a men's size 6 or a women's size 7–8 shoe. You radio dispatch to request that a crime scene technician be deployed to the scene to process it and help collect evidence. You and Officer Blacksmith then move to the back of the building, where you observe that the back door is slightly open.

One of the department's Crime Scene Investigation (CSI) technicians, Jim Harris, arrives at approximately 10:00 p.m. At approximately 10:05 p.m., Kevin Peterson, the owner of Peterson's Jewelers, arrives. You and Officer Blacksmith take down his personal information while CSI Technician Harris processes the scene outside of the store. Mr. Peterson is a White male and his date of birth is September 24, 1963. He resides at 526 Gray Sands Avenue, Lovettsville, Michigan.

His telephone number is 401-623-9455 and his driver's license number is 01-2234-89. CSI Technician Harris takes photographs of the recycling bin and broken window, takes casts of the shoe prints, and dusts the window and back door for latent prints. When he completes these tasks, he informs you, Officer Blacksmith, and Mr. Peterson that is okay to enter the store.

You, Officer Blacksmith, Mr. Peterson, and Technician Harris enter through the door at the back of the store. You immediately notice a large brick on the floor below the broken window. There is also shattered glass on the floor. Technician Harris begins to photograph the scene and dust for footprints. You, Officer Blacksmith, and Mr. Peterson walk toward the front of the store to see what, if anything, is missing from the display cases. One of the display cases has been pried open. Mr. Peterson reports the following jewelry missing: (1) a men's Movado watch (silver case and band), (2) a 1-carat blue sapphire pendant with a 14-karat 16" gold chain, (3) a men's 24-karat gold link bracelet, and (4) a 24-karat gold diamond solitaire ring with a 0.5-carat princess-cut diamond. Technician Harris comes to the front of the store and takes photographs of the display case and dusts it for latent prints.

According to Mr. Peterson, the total value of the stolen jewelry is $4,700. This includes: $800 for the Movado watch, $750 for the sapphire necklace, $450 for the men's gold bracelet, and $2,700 for the diamond ring.

As you and Officer Blacksmith return to the parking lot of the store, a man approaches you. He says that he lives across the street from Peterson's Jewelers. He tells you that his name is Jefferson Miller and that he lives at 3531 North Avenue. His telephone number is 401-838-8977. He is African American, his date of birth is January 8, 1950, and he is a retired postal worker. His driver's license number is 44-4553-59. Mr. Miller tells you that he saw a blue van leaving the store parking lot at about 9:30 p.m.

Investigative Statements

You take a statement from Kevin Peterson. He states that he closed the store at about 8:00 p.m. after having a fairly slow day. He states that a man and a woman, whom he had never seen before, came in and told him they wanted to look at engagement rings. He further states that the two were polite and seemed very interested in buying one of the rings (the one that was subsequently stolen). However, the man (whom the woman called "Tiny") told Mr. Peterson that they would have to think about it but would probably be back. Mr. Peterson describes the man as White, in his late 20s, with very short, spiky blond hair, and blue eyes. He further describes the man as thin and not very tall, with a chipped front tooth. He thinks that one of his eyebrows may have been pierced. According to Mr. Peterson, the young man was wearing black cargo shorts and a white Detroit Lions t-shirt.

Mr. Peterson then describes the young woman. He states she was African American, in her late 20s, had long dreadlocks, and blue eyes. He also states that she was thin and had a scar on her left hand, which he noticed when she tried on the rings. The woman was wearing a blue "summery" skirt and a yellow top. Both the man and the woman wore tennis shoes.

Mr. Peterson states that when the couple left the store, they got into a blue van with Michigan license plates. He did not see what direction the car went when it left the parking lot.

Witness Statements

Officer Blacksmith takes a statement from Jefferson Miller who states that he saw a blue van leaving the parking lot of Peterson's Jewelers at about 9:30 p.m. on the night of the burglary. He is unable to provide an exact description of the people in the car, but confirms that there were two people in the vehicle and he believes one person was female. Mr. Miller states that he took his dog out for a walk around the block after he finished watching his 9:00 television show. As he turned the corner onto North Avenue, he saw the blue van leaving the parking lot of Peterson's but did not think anything about it because cars frequently use the parking lot as a turn-around point.

Preparing Professional Reports and Presentations, Handout #1

Mr. Miller then states that when he saw the police officers at the store, he realized that he should report what he had seen.

Offense Information
Case number: 03-9087
Code Section and Description: GS 12-52—Breaking or Entering Buildings Generally; GS 32-46—Felony Theft

Officer Information
Officer Number: ID #878, Division 03
Approved by: Sgt. Mark Peters, ID #323
Detective Assigned: Lisa Brinton, ID #125, Division 03
Date and Time of Report: July 15, 2015, 11:00 a.m.
Case Station: Downtown
Agency: Lovettsville Police Department

Preparing Professional Reports and Presentations, Handout #2

Incident Report

Incident Report		☐ Crime ☐ Incident ☐ Person ☐ Property ☐ Miscellaneous

Incident #	Incident/ Offense	Date Occurred - MM/DD/YY	Time Occurred	Date Reported- MM/DD/YY	Time reported
Location of Offense/ Incident		Location Code	Location Type	Type of Weapon/ Tool Used	Case #

PERSONS INVOLVED (Victims / Witnesses)

NAME AND ADDRESS	DOB	RACE	SEX	TELEPHONE
Last Name, First, Middle Initial				HOME
Number, Street, Apt. #, City and State				
Last Name, First, Middle Initial				HOME
Number, Street, Apt. #, City and State				

PERSONS INVOLVED (Suspects)

NAME AND ADDRESS	DOB	RACE	SEX	TELEPHONE
Last Name, First, Middle Initial				HOME
Number, Street, Apt. #, City and State				
Description				HOME
Last Name, First, Middle Initial				
Number, Street, Apt. #, City and State				
Description				

ITEMS TAKEN

NAME OF ITEM	
SERIAL NO.	VALUE
NAME OF ITEM	
SERIAL NO.	VALUE
NAME OF ITEM	
SERIAL NO.	VALUE
NAME OF ITEM	
SERIAL NO.	VALUE
NAME OF ITEM	
SERIAL NO.	VALUE
NAME OF ITEM	
SERIAL NO.	VALUE

Narrative

_____
_____
_____
_____
_____

Narrative (cont'd)

Narrative (cont'd)

Preparing Professional Reports and Presentations, Handout #3

Preparing a Risk Assessment System–Community Supervision Screening Tool (RAS-CSST)

RISK ASSESSMENT SYSTEM - COMMUNITY SUPERVISION SCREENING TOOL (RAS-CSST)

Name: _____ Date of Assessment: _____

APR #: _____ Probation Officer: _____

1.0 Number of Prior Adult Felony Convictions
    0 = None
    1 = One or Two
    2 = Three or more

2.0 Number of Prior Juvenile Convictions
    0 = None
    1 = One or Two
    2 = Three or more

3.0 Currently Employed
    0 = Yes, Full-Time, Disabled or Retired
    1 = Not Employed, or Employed Part-Time

4.0 Drugs Readily Available in Neighborhood
    0 = No, Generally Not Available
    1 = Yes, Somewhat Available
    2 = Yes, Easily Available

5.0 Mental Health Issues
   0 = None
   1 = Depression
   2 = Substance Abuse (Drugs and/or Alcohol)

6.0 Criminal Friends
   0 = None
   1 = Some
   2 = Majority

7.0 Criminal Family
   0 = None
   1 = Some
   2 = Majority

TOTAL

Scores	Ratings	Supervision
0 - 5	Low	Community Supervision
6 - 9	Medium	Intensive Supervision
10 - 13	High	Pre-Trial Detention

Recommendations (type of supervision, type of services)

_____
_____
_____
_____

Preparing Professional Reports and Presentations, Handout #4

Child Protective Services: A Case Study

Child Protective Services Scenario

You are a Child Protective Services case manager. On Friday, March 25, 2016, at 10:30 a.m., you receive a call from Jennifer Goode who says she is calling because she is worried that a little boy who lives next door to her is being abused by his father. She tells you that this is the first time she has called about this, but that she has been worried about him "for some time." She tells you that her neighbors are Russell and Tami Schwartz, and their son's name is Jack. The Schwartzes live at 634 Pershing Court, Lovettsville, Michigan. They are Caucasian. Russell is approximately 40 years old, Tami is approximately 35 years old, and Jack is 8 years old. Their telephone number is 555-332-9189.

Investigative Statement

According to Jennifer Goode, she picked up Jack the previous afternoon at the bus stop. Jack is in second grade at Emerick Elementary School. Ms. Goode states that she often picks up Jack when Tami Schwartz has to work late at her day care job at The Learning Tree. Ms. Goode further states that when Jack got into the car, she was surprised to see that he had a cast on his left wrist, because it was the same wrist he had broken the previous year. When she asked him about it, he said that he had fallen out of a tree in his backyard. Ms. Goode found this strange, because his mother had recently told her that when they had gone to the fair, Jack refused to ride on the Ferris wheel because he was afraid of heights.

Ms. Goode further states that the broken wrist also "raised a red flag" because she has often seen bruises on Jack's arms and legs. On two occasions, he appeared to have a hard time getting into her car, as though his legs hurt him when he moved. All of these incidents occurred immediately after his father had gotten home from business trips.

Ms. Goode is also concerned about Jack's mother, Tami Schwartz. She states that she has seen bruises on Mrs. Schwartz as well, and that Mrs. Schwartz and her husband argue frequently. Ms. Goode reports that the previous week, she saw two police officers knocking on the Schwartzes' door after she had heard the couple arguing. She says the police were at the house for about 30 minutes. She does not think anyone was arrested.

Ms. Goode also states that the police were at the Schwartzes' house last July during a family barbeque. Ms. Goode says that she was having dinner on her deck during their party and saw that Russell Schwartz was very inebriated. At one point, he got into a verbal altercation with Tami Schwartz's brother-in-law that escalated into a physical fight. Ms. Goode does not know the brother-in-law's name, but she believes he is married to Tami Schwartz's sister Susan, who lives in Shorewood, a neighboring town. Ms. Goode believes that Susan called the police but she is not certain. Ms. Goode states that the police were at the Schwartz house for about half an hour, but that, as far as she knows, no arrests were made. She also reports that this was not the first time she has seen Russell Schwartz drunk. She also saw him under the influence at the neighborhood block party that summer. She believes that Russell Schwartz may have a problem with alcohol but she does not believe that Tami Schwartz drinks.

Ms. Goode states that she decided to call Child Protective Services today and report her suspicions about Russell Schwartz, because on the previous evening, when she was in her backyard, she saw and heard Russell and Tami Schwartz arguing on the back deck of their house. When the argument became "really heated," Tami Schwartz ran into her house and slammed the door. Russell Schwartz followed her into the house, where the yelling continued. In addition, this morning when Ms. Goode went out to pick up her newspaper, she saw Tami Schwartz, who was taking out her trash. Ms. Goode asked Mrs. Schwartz about Jack's wrist. According to Ms. Goode, Tami Schwartz "acted very strangely" and hurried back into her house. Ms. Goode states that this, in combination with the previous evening's argument, has "gotten her really worried." She does not worry as much about Jack's overall health, because he always appears to be well fed, but she is very worried about the possibility of physical abuse.

Jennifer Goode reports that she has lived next to the Schwartzes for approximately six years and has gotten to know Tami and Jack Schwartz well because she and Mrs. Schwartz talk often "over their shared fence" when Russell Schwartz is away on business. Ms. Goode believes Russell Schwartz works for Citibank and that he travels at least three weeks out of every month. Ms. Goode states that she enjoys having the Schwartzes as next-door-neighbors, because their house is always well maintained. She is very fond of Jack, who is "a sweet boy, very polite, and well dressed." Ms. Goode also says that both Tami and Jack Schwartz seem "really happy" when Russell Schwartz is away, spending a lot of time playing various games in the backyard and having barbeques with Tami Schwartz's sister Susan. However, when Russell Schwartz is home, they all stay inside and Susan does not visit.

Jennifer Goode's address is 636 Pershing Court, Lovettsville, Michigan. Her telephone number is 555-332-7823. Pershing Court is located 3 miles past Emerick Elementary School, in a cul-de-sac on the left-hand side of the street.

Intake Information
Screening Decision: In
Assigned to: Linda Falls, Frederick County; Friday, March 25, 2016, at 4:30 p.m.
Confirmed with: Sandra Smith
Assessment: None at this time
Case Name: Schwartz
Case Number: FHJ-12891
Report Involves: Request for assistance

Preparing Professional Reports and Presentations, Handout #5

Preparing Professional Reports and Presentations, Handout #5

Preparing a Child Protective Services Intake Form

CPS Intake Form	Date: _____ Time: _____
	Screened by: (Name) _____ (County) _____
	Screening Decision: In _____ Out _____ Referred Due to Residency _____
	Assigned to: (County/Worker Name) _____
	Referred to: (County Name) _____ Date/Time _____
	            Confirmed with _____
	            Was Safety Assessed: ___ Yes (Date) _____ By _____
	                            ___ No Reason _____
	Type of Report: Abuse _____ Neglect _____ Dependency _____
	If referring to another county for assessment, do not complete the information below:
	        Family Assessment _____ Investigative Assessment _____
	Initiation Response Time: Immediate _____ 24 Hours _____ 72 Hours _____
	Case Name: _____ Case Number: _____
	This report involves: ☐ Conflict of Interest ☐ Out of Home Placement ☐ Request for Assistance

Family Information	Children's Information Relationship to Alleged Perpetrator Name (include nicknames) Sex Race Age/DOB School/Child Care A. B. _____ _____ _____ _____ _____ Parent/Caretaker's Information Name (include aliases/nicknames) Sex Race Age/DOB Employment/School _____ _____ _____ Alleged Perpetrator's Information Name (include aliases/nicknames) Sex Race Age/DOB Employment/School A. _____ B. _____ Other household members Name (include aliases/nicknames) Sex Race Age/DOB Employment/School _____ _____ _____ Address & phone number of all household members, including the length of time at current address, include former addresses if family is new to the area: _____ _____ _____ Family's primary language: _____ Driving Directions: _____ _____ Others who may have knowledge of the situation (include name, address and phone number) _____ _____ Do you have any information about the children's other maternal and paternal relatives? (Include name, address, telephone number) _____ _____ Has the family ever been involved with this agency or any other community agency? Do you know of other reports made about the family? _____ _____

Family Information

What happened to the child(ren), in simple terms?

Did you see physical evidence of abuse or neglect? If yes, please describe.

Is there anything that makes you believe the child(ren) is/are in immediate danger?

Has there been any occurrence of domestic violence in the home?

Are you concerned about a family member's drug/alcohol use?

Approximately when did the incident occur?

When is the last time you saw the child(ren)?

Current location of child(ren), parent/caretaker, perpetrator?

How do you know what happened with the family?

How long has this been going on?

Safety Factors

Are you aware of any safety problems with a social worker going to the home? If so, what?

Calling DSS is a big step, what do you think can be done with the family to make the child(ren) safer?

Is there anything you can do to help the family?

Has anything happened recently that prompted you to call today?

Preparing Professional Reports and Presentations, Handout #5

Physical Abuse	Where was the child(ren) when the abuse occurred?
	Describe the injury, for example (Thursday, May 23, 2012, a.m. or p.m., red and blue mark, 1" by 4" shaped like a belt mark, fresh or fading)
	What part of the body was injured?
	Is there a need for medical treatment?
	What is the parent/caretaker's explanation?
	What is the child(ren)'s explanation?
	What led to the child(ren)'s disclosure or brought the child(ren) to your attention?
	Did anyone witness the abuse?
	Are any family members taking protective action?
	Have you had previous concerns about the family?
	Is/Are the child(ren) currently afraid of the alleged perpetrator?
	Is/Are the child(ren) afraid to go home?
Emotional Abuse	How does the child(ren) function in school?
	What symptoms does this child(ren) have that would indicate psychological, emotional, social impairment?
	Are there any psychological or psychiatric evaluations of the child(ren)?
	Is the child(ren) failing to thrive or developmentally delayed?
	Is there a bond between the parent/caretaker and child(ren)?
	What has the parent/caretaker done that is harmful?
	How long has the situation been going on, and what changes have been observed?
	Are there any indications of cruel and unusual punishment?

Domestic Violence	Has anyone in the family been hurt or assaulted? If so, describe the assault or harm (what and when). If so, who has been hurt? Who is hurting the child and other family members? Please describe the injuries specifically.
	Can you describe how the violence is affecting the child(ren)?
	Have the police ever been called to the house to stop assaults against either the adults or child(ren)? Was anyone arrested? Were charges filed?
	Where is the child(ren) when the violent incidents occur?
	Has any family member stalked another family member? Has a family member taken another family member hostage?
	Do you know who is caring for and protecting the child(ren) right now?
	What is the battered parent/caretaker's ability to protect him/herself and the child(ren)?
	What steps were taken to prevent the perpetrator's access to the home? (shelter, police, restraining order)
	Is there a history of domestic violence?
	Can you provide information on how to contact the battered parent/caretaker alone?
Substance Abuse	What specific drugs are being used by the parent/caretaker?
	What is the frequency of use?
	Do the child(ren) have knowledge of the drug use?
	How does their substance use affect their ability to care for the child(ren)?
	Are there drugs, legal or illegal in the home? If so, where are they located?
	Do the child(ren) have access to the drugs?
	Has the parent ever experienced black outs?
	How well are the child(ren) supervised? Are they left alone for extended periods of time?

Preparing Professional Reports and Presentations, Handout #5

Injurious Environment	What is it about the child(ren)'s living environment that makes it unsafe?
Improper Discipline	If the child(ren) is injured from the discipline, please describe the injuries in specific detail; also describe any instrument used to discipline.
	Does the parent/caretaker have a pattern of disciplining inappropriately?
	Is the child(ren) fearful of the parent/caretaker?
	Do you know what prompted the parent/caretaker to discipline the child(ren)?
Reporter Information	Reporter's name, address, telephone number, relationship to family:
	Reporter waives right to notification? Yes ☐ No ☐
	Is the reporter available to provide further information if needed? Yes ☐ No ☐
Maltreatment Screening Tool	Indicate which of the following screening tools were consulted in the screening of this report: Abuse: Physical Injury _____ Cruel/Grossly Inappropriate Behavior Modification _____ Sexual Abuse _____ Emotional Abuse _____ Moral Turpitude _____ Neglect: Improper Care _____ Improper Supervision _____ Improper Discipline _____ Abandonment _____ Improper Medical/Remedial Care _____ Injurious Environment _____ Illegal Placement/Adoption _____ Dependency _____ Substance Abuse _____ Domestic Violence _____
Response Priority Decision Tree	After consulting the appropriate Maltreatment Screening Tool(s), if the decision is to accept the report, then consult the Response Priority Decision Tree. Indicate which of the following Response Priority Decision Trees were consulted and the response required (immediate, 24 hours, 72 hours). Physical Abuse _____ Sexual Abuse _____ Moral Turpitude _____ Neglect _____ Dependency _____ Emotional Abuse _____
Signatures	A two-level review was given by: (Include name, position, and date)

Preparing Professional Reports and Presentations, Take-Home Assignment #1

Preparing an Incident Report

Read the information contained in *Preparing Professional Reports and Presentations, Handout #1: "Crime Scene Report: A Case Study."* Then, using the information contained in that handout and the guidelines you learned in this unit, complete *Preparing Professional Reports and Presentations, Handout #2: "Incident Report."*

Note! If you type your narrative into an editable .pdf version of this report, the text will not wrap around at the end of each line as it does when you type a paragraph in a Word document. Therefore, you should pay careful attention to the amount of text you enter on each line; if you enter too much, it will be cut off.

Preparing Professional Reports and Presentations, Take-Home Assignment #2

Preparing a Risk Assessment System–Community Supervision Screening Tool (RAS-CSST)

Read the information contained in *Preparing Professional Reports and Presentations, Handout #1: "Crime Scene Report: A Case Study."* Then, using the information contained in that handout and the guidelines you learned in this unit, complete *Preparing Professional Reports and Presentations, Handout #3: "Preparing a Risk Assessment System–Community Supervision Screening Tool (RAS-CSST).*

Note! If you type your narrative into an editable .pdf version of this report, the text will not wrap around at the end of each line as it does when you type a paragraph in a Word document. Therefore, you should pay careful attention to the amount of text you enter on each line; if you enter too much, it will be cut off.

When you fill out the assessment, follow these instructions:

1. In the top section of the assessment, fill in the subject's name, the current date, a fictional APR # (case number), and your name as the assigned probation officer. For this assessment, your subject will be Thomas Kennedy, who was the suspect in the crime scene scenario.

2. Using a "weighted" scoring system (e.g., 0, 1, 2, 3), score each item on the instrument. For items #1, #2, #3, and #6, use the information provided in the crime scene scenario to assign a score for each item. For the remaining items, determine a score based on what you infer from the scenario.

3. After you have scored all seven items, add them up and record a total score. Use the rating system at the bottom of the page to classify Thomas Kennedy into one of three risk categories for reoffending (e.g., low, medium, high). Based on his total score, write a recommendation for Thomas Kennedy. In it, include the appropriate level of supervision for him and the services you would recommend be incorporated into his case plan to address his "criminogenic needs."

Preparing Professional Reports and Presentations, Take-Home Assignment #3

Preparing a Child Protective Services Intake Form

Read the information contained in *Preparing Professional Reports and Presentations, Handout #4, "Child Protective Services: A Case Study."* Then, using the information contained in the handout and the guidelines you learned in this unit, complete *Preparing Professional Reports and Presentations, Handout #5, "Preparing a Child Protective Services Intake Form."*

Note! If you type your narrative into an editable .pdf version of this report, the text will not wrap around at the end of each line as it does when you type a paragraph in a Word document. Therefore, you should pay careful attention to the amount of text you enter on each line; if you enter too much, it will be cut off.

References

Adams, S. (2013, February 5). *New survey: LinkedIn more dominant than ever among job seekers and recruiters, but Facebook poised to gain.* Retrieved from http://www.forbes.com/sites/susan-adams/2013/02/05/new-survey-linked-in-more-dominant-than-ever-among-job-seekers-and-recruiters-but-facebook-poised-to-gain/#195ffb8816bf.

American Psychological Association. (2010). *Publication manual of the American Psychological Association, Sixth Edition.* Washington, DC: Author.

Bonta, J. (2002). Offender risk assessment: Guidelines for selection and use. *Criminal Justice and Behavior, 29*(4), 355–379.

Carlton, J. (2011, January 4). Texan declared innocent after 30 years in prison. *Associated Press.* Retrieved from http://www.msnbc.msn.com/id/40909822

Child Welfare Information Gateway. (n.d.). *Overview.* Retrieved from https://www.childwelfare.gov

College Examination Entrance Board. (2004, September). *Writing: A ticket to work . . . or a ticket out. A survey of business leaders* (Report of the National Commission on Writing). New York: Author.

Espinel, V. (2011, March 15). Concrete steps Congress can take to protect America's intellectual property [Web log post]. Retrieved from http://www.whitehouse.gov/blog/2011/03/15/concrete-steps-congress-can-take-protect-americas-intellectual-property

Etter, G. W., Sr., & Birzer, M. L. (2007). Domestic violence abusers: A descriptive study of the characteristics of defenders in protection from abuse orders in Sedgwick County, Kansas. *Journal of Family Violence, 22,* 113–119. doi: 10.1007/s10896-006-9047-x

Ferree, C. W. (2006). *DUI recidivism and attorney type: Is there a connection?* (Unpublished master's thesis). University of Baltimore, Baltimore, MD.

Hoots, G. A. (2014). *The importance of quality report writing.* Retrieved from http://www.cji.edu/site/assets/files/1921/the-importance-of-quality-reportwriting-in-law-enforcement.pdf

James, N. (2015). *Risk and needs assessment in the criminal justice system.* Washington, DC: Congressional Research Service.

Jobvite. (2014). *2014 social recruiting survey*. Retrieved from https://timedotcom.files.wordpress.com/2014/09/jobvite_socialrecruiting_survey2014.pdf

LinkedIn. (2016). *Company info*. Retrieved from https://www.linkedin.com/about-us?trk=hb_ft_about

Liu, S., Siegel, P. Z., Brewer, R. D., Mokdad, A. H., Sleet, D. A., & Serdula, M. (1997). Prevalence of alcohol-impaired driving: Results from a national self-reported survey of health behaviors. *Journal of the American Medical Association, 277*(2), 122–125.

McCabe, D. L., Trevino, L. K., & Butterfield, K. D. (2001). Cheating in academic institutions: A decade of research. *Ethics & Behavior, 11,* 219–232.

McMullen, L. (2015, February 19). *What recruiters think when they see your LinkedIn profile*. Retrieved from http://money.usnews.com/money/careers/articles/2015/02/19/what-recruiters-think-when-they-see-your-linkedin-profile

Mulford, C., & Giordano, P. C. (2008). Teen dating violence: A closer look at adolescent romantic relationships. *NIJ Journal, 261,* 34–40. Retrieved from http://www.nij.gov/journals/261/pages/teen-dating-violence.aspx

Number of employers passing on applicants due to social media posts continues to rise. (2014, June 26). *CareerBuilder.com*. Retrieved from http://www.careerbuilder.com/share/aboutus/pressreleasesdetail.aspx?sd=6%2F26%2F2014&id=pr829&ed=12%2F31%2F2014

Office for Victims of Crime (2003). *Community outreach through police in schools* (OVC Bulletin). Washington, DC: U.S. Department of Justice.

Office of Juvenile Justice Delinquency Prevention. (2015, June). *Drug courts*. Washington, DC: Office of Justice Programs, U.S. Department of Justice.

Oudekerk B., Blachman-Demner, D., & Mulford, C. (2014, November). *Teen dating violence: How peers can affect risk & protective factors* (Research in Brief). Washington, DC: National Institute of Justice.

Parker, K., Lenhart, A., & Moore, K. (2011). *The digital revolution and higher education. College presidents and public differ on value of online learning*. Retrieved from http://www.pewsocialtrends.org/files/2011/08/online-learning.pdf

Rape, Abuse, and Incest National Network. (2009). *Reporting rates*. Retrieved from http://www.rainn.org/get-information/statistics/reporting-rates

Rosenmerkel, S., Durose, M., & Farole, D., Jr. (2009). *Felony sentences in state courts, 2006—Statistical tables* (National Judicial Reporting Program). Washington, DC: Bureau of Justice Statistics, U.S. Department of Justice.

The Muse (n.d.). *How to write a cover letter: 31 tips you need to know*. Retrieved from https://www.themuse.com/advice/how-to-write-a-cover-letter-31-tips-you-need-to-know

References

Truman, J. L., & Langton, L. (2014, September). *Criminal victimization, 2013* (Bulletin 247648). Washington, DC: Bureau of Justice Statistics, U.S. Department of Justice.

U.S. Census Bureau, Population Division. (2014). Retrieved from http://www.census.gov/population/projections/data/national/2014/summarytables.html

Visher, C., Kachnowski, V., La Vigne, N., & Travis, J. (2004). *Baltimore prisoners' experiences returning home*. Washington, DC: Urban Institute.

Zweig, J. M., Dank, M., Lachman, P., & Yahner, J. (2013, July). *Technology, teen dating violence and abuse, and bullying.* Retrieved from http://www.nij.gov/publications/pages/publicationdetail.aspx?ncjnumber=243296